SEVEN MINUTES — *with* — JESUS for New Believers

Guidance for Your First Steps in Faith

A 60-Day Devotional

RAY CUMMINGS

WHITAKER HOUSE

Boldface type in Scripture quotations and other citations indicates the author's emphasis, not boldface in the original text.

SEVEN MINUTES WITH JESUS FOR NEW BELIEVERS
Guidance for Your First Steps in Faith (A 60-Day Devotional)

Ray Cummings
Raycummings1970@icloud.com

ISBN: 979-8-88769-606-5 | eBook ISBN: 979-8-88769-607-2
Printed in the United States of America

Whitaker House
1030 Hunt Valley Circle | New Kensington, PA 15068
www.whitakerhouse.com

Library of Congress Cataloging-in-Publication Data
LC record available at https://lccn.loc.gov/2025037062
LC ebook record available at https://lccn.loc.gov/2025037063

1 2 3 4 5 6 7 8 9 10 11 33 32 31 30 29 28 27 26

CONTENTS

Endorsements for *Seven Minutes with Jesus for New Believers:*

As President of Commissioned International, I've walked through mountain villages in Central America and across the globe, meeting new believers who long for a resource to help build a strong spiritual foundation. *Seven Minutes with Jesus for New Believers* is exactly that. This book offers a practical and accessible framework for growth in Christ—one that transcends borders and cultures. I wholeheartedly commend it as a vital tool for new believers in the United States, Central America, and around the world.

—*Timmy Ruhnke*
President, Commissioned International

Taking time to meet with Jesus changes everything. In *Seven Minutes with Jesus for New Believers,* Dr. Ray Cummings provides a simple yet powerful guide to help us begin our journey with God. Every marathon begins with a single step—maybe your life with God will start with just seven minutes, but it won't stay there. This devotional will help you deepen your relationship with Jesus, understand God's will, and walk faithfully with Him each day. So, why not start with seven minutes?

—*Luiz Cardoso*
Senior Pastor, Glasgow Story Church
Leader, Project Scotland

Seven Minutes with Jesus for New Believers is the perfect companion for those beginning their walk with Christ. Dr. Ray Cummings writes with the heart of a pastor and the wisdom of a seasoned disciple-maker.

As a pastor, I have consistently sought practical, biblical resources to help people start their faith journey. If you're looking for a resource to help someone take those crucial early steps after salvation, *Seven Minutes with Jesus for New Believers* is it! Dr. Cummings distills bite-sized truths from Scripture into concise devotions that are both easy to read and rich in application. This devotional is a must-have for anyone wanting to build a strong foundation of faith. Biblical. Inspirational. Practical! I highly recommend this book for churches, mentors, and anyone discipling new believers.

—*Dr. Scott Hanberry*
Executive Director, Homes of Hope for Children

I want to thank Pastor Ray Cummings for providing us with something of great value, especially for those who have recently experienced new life in Christ. I encourage every pastor to consider using *Seven Minutes with Jesus for New Believers* in their churches. Every new believer will benefit from a journey through this timely devotional. I am convinced that God will use this book to help believers grow spiritually.

—*Roberto Sequeira*
Missionary, BMDMI—Managua, Nicaragua

As a pastor's kid and as a staff pastor for fifteen years, I know firsthand that leading people to Jesus is usually the easy part. Discipling them, which is so essential, is a significantly more challenging task. My friend, Dr. Ray Cummings, has created an amazing guide to help people move toward discipleship. From prayer and Bible study, to building community with fellow believers, to growing in your faith, Dr. Cummings leads you through sixty easy-to-understand, step-by-step, real-life devotionals—in only seven minutes each day! I highly recommend *Seven Minutes with Jesus for New Believers* for any Christian who wants to deepen their walk with the Lord. I think it would be an excellent idea for every church to have a stack of them to share with every new convert.

—*Geron Davis*
Songwriter/Worship Leader, Holy Ground Ministries

PREFACE

This resource is designed for new believers as a tool for discipleship. The intent behind *Seven Minutes with Jesus for New Believers* is to help Christians begin their journey with Jesus, studying God's Word while focusing on discipleship.

To become Jesus's disciple, you need someone to walk alongside you as an encouraging mentor. Scripture teaches this not only as a means of accountability but also as necessary for spiritual growth. (See Titus 2:1–6.) Prayerfully consider who can walk with you through these crucial first steps in your newly found journey with Jesus. Find someone of the same gender who is a mature Christian, give them a copy of this book, and ask them to meet with you once a week for the next eight weeks.

You can download a free study guide to facilitate your weekly meetings at **sevenminuteswithjesus.com.** In this study guide, you will find seven questions to consider each week that will take what you are learning to a deeper application point in your life.

Over the last few months, I have come to realize that questions are the key to discipleship. I was shocked to discover that the Gospels record 307 questions asked by Jesus. What is even more intriguing is that Jesus was asked 183 questions, yet He only answered three of them.[1] You would think that Jesus would give direct answers to people's questions. Yet, many times, He responded to questions by asking questions of His own.

Jesus asked questions to allow people to wrestle with what they were learning. Christ wants us to apply His truth to our daily lives, so He employs questions to help people understand how to live out what they are learning. Consider the following:

Information without Investigation leads to Stagnation.

Information with Investigation leads to Transformation.

Therefore, it is vitally important as you begin this new life in Christ that you take the time to investigate God's truths by walking through questions with seasoned Christians.

I am praying for your new journey, that God will bring you from a decisive commitment in Christ to a life of discipleship with Him!

INTRODUCTION

"Since you are reading this, that means someone just died." Perhaps you have heard that in a movie before. Yet this is not a scene from a film, but it could be the making of a masterpiece. Since you are reading this, that means you have died to self, so that you could repent of your sins and trust in Jesus Christ as your Lord and Savior. That is the greatest decision anyone could ever make, and I expect you have made that life-changing commitment since you are holding this book in your hands or reading the e-book version. That means you are on the journey to become more like Jesus Christ, which is known as discipleship. This is the most important commitment, which leads to the most incredible journey, because it comes with the most significant relationship that anyone could have—a personal relationship with Jesus Christ. This journey is ecstatic and eternal. So welcome to the family of faith and the journey of discipleship!

First and foremost, God's desire is to save you into an ongoing relationship with Him. The following statement may be startling, but it is true. God's goal for your life is not that you just decide to believe in Him. That is just the starting point. God's Word indicates that He wants you to become a fully devoted follower. Christ desires that you follow Him and become His disciple. Decisions are made in a day, but discipleship is a process that takes time. After your decision that led to your salvation, the goal of this book and the purpose of this sixty-day devotional is to help you start your journey toward discipleship.

As we begin, we must answer a few questions. First, why seven minutes? Can less than one percent of your day profoundly impact your life?

To answer those questions, let's look at what can happen in seven minutes. The International Space Station travels approximately 2,000 miles in seven minutes. The average human body produces 1.6 billion new cells in seven minutes. The Earth can travel almost 8,400 miles while orbiting the Sun in seven minutes. What can happen in seven minutes is determined by the amount of power behind you. Is there anything or anyone more powerful than God? Absolutely not. Without question, no one or nothing is mightier than our God. What would happen if you spent seven minutes daily in God's Word? The possibilities are limitless.

Please don't misinterpret the title of this devotional series. I strongly encourage you to spend more than seven minutes with Jesus daily. However, seven minutes is simply the length of time it will take to read each day's devotion. Throughout your day, God will remind you of each day's Scripture and devotional thoughts as you grow in your relationship with Him. Not to mention, there is an ongoing conversation in prayer with God that is always available to every believer.[2]

Why a sixty-day devotional? I have always heard that it takes twenty-one days to form a habit. I recently discovered that experts believe this myth resulted from a 1960 self-help book by a plastic surgeon named Maxwell Maltz. In his book, Maxwell observed that it took his patients about twenty-one days to get used to their new appearance after surgery. So, the origin of the three-week theory of developing a habit had nothing to do with habits, per se. After this book was written, others also set three weeks as the time needed for people to form a habit, and the rest is repetition of misinformation.

Over sixty years later, recent studies have produced strong evidence that refutes this idea. Studies have now revealed that developing a habit takes an average of sixty days. Of course, some people cultivate habits faster, while others take more time. Yet, sixty days is the average.[3]

This daily devotional is strategically built to support your spiritual growth. Each day consists of the following:

- Scripture reading: a passage of Scripture from God's Word
- Explanation: key insights and biblically grounded concepts for new believers
- Application: thought-provoking questions for you to ponder by yourself or with others in a small group
- Prayer: a prompt to help you begin your daily prayer time with God

I am so excited about this sixty-day, sustainable, habit-forming devotional that can radically move your discipleship journey in the right direction. So, let's get going and grow with Jesus!

Part 1

A REAL RELATIONSHIP WITH JESUS

At the exact moment you placed your faith in Jesus Christ for salvation, you entered into a dynamic relationship with God. This relationship is just as real as any of your other relationships. While you can't see Jesus, you can still experience Him. Like any other relationship, your union with Christ strengthens the longer you are together.

In your relationship with God, don't simply think of Him as sitting way up in heaven on His throne. Realize He is a God who makes Himself known. He is King and Lord and should be revered and worshipped accordingly. But He is also a relational God. He didn't save you so that you could spend eternity with Him in heaven when you die. He saved you to have a growing relationship with Him now.

Like any relationship, you need a foundation to build upon. In the next seven days, we will examine what you were saved from and for. You will learn that you can experience God's power and know His love, which can build confidence and drive out any of your fears. God has a purpose for your life that He wishes to make known through a relationship with you.

Unlike any other relationship, God is with you every second, 24/7–365 days a year. Remember, while you can't see Him, He is always there. In fact, by the power of the Holy Spirit, He lives inside of you!

Day 1

WHAT WAS I SAVED FROM?

Scripture Reading: Romans 6:23

> *For the wages of sin is death, but the free gift of God is eternal life through Christ Jesus our Lord.*

Explanation:

Thank you for joining us in this devotional study for new believers. Before discussing what we have been saved for, we must focus on what we were saved from. Never forgetting why God saved you can help you fully appreciate what your salvation involves.

Scripture declares that the payment for our sin is death. Just as a worker earns his wages, sinners deserve spiritual death and separation from God. Romans 3:23 affirms that we are all sinners. So, before anyone ever started on a journey with Jesus, every person was on a pathway leading to death.

Dead people can do nothing for themselves. For life to occur, they desperately need a miracle. For that to happen, they need Someone with the power over death to intervene and bring them back to life. Salvation starts with Jesus sharing His resurrection power in your life. Even the faith we place in Jesus must come from Him because we are spiritually dead. Without Him, we are helpless and hopeless. Yet with Him, all things are possible.

That's why a person born twice can only die once, and a person born once will die twice. If you have been spiritually born again, along with your physical birth, you will only experience a physical death. However, if a person was never born again spiritually, then they will eventually die a physical death. When that time comes, they will also be dead spiritually, because that person was never made alive by Jesus Christ.

Contrasting the earned wages of sin, Romans 6:23 continues with these words, *"but the free gift of God is eternal life through Jesus Christ our Lord."* Death is an earned consequence of sin, while salvation is a free gift from God.

In the introduction, you read these words: "Since you are reading this, that means someone just died." Oddly enough, if you resist trusting in Jesus for salvation, you will have to pay the wages of sin, which is death. However, if you turn from your selfish ways by dying to yourself, and admitting you are a sinner, God can save you and grant you forgiveness of sin and eternal life. When Jesus died on the cross, He paid the wages for the sin that we owed. We are all going to experience death. The question is, when and how? Either we die to self and receive God's gift of salvation, or we die in our sins and have to pay the wages for our own sin.

Since you are reading this book, I presume you have already accepted Jesus's payment for your sins. Never forget what Christ saved you from. Jesus paid the ultimate price for your sin so you could be resurrected to eternal life. Live daily with gratitude that He has rescued you from spiritual death!

Application:

How can your journey with Jesus be a continual "Thank You" for Him saving you from death to life?

Prayer:

Thank You, Jesus, for all that You have done, so that I could receive the gift of salvation. Please help me to live daily fully aware of what You saved me from...

Day 2

WHAT AM I SAVED FOR?

Scripture Reading: Ephesians 2:8–10 (NKJV)

> *For by grace you have been saved through faith, and that not of yourselves; it is the gift of God, not of works, lest anyone should boast. For we are His workmanship, created in Christ Jesus for good works, which God prepared beforehand that we should walk in them.*

Explanation:

Ephesians 2:8 reinforces the claim made in Romans 6:23 that salvation is a gift from God. That gift is received by faith. You opened that gift the moment you experienced salvation. The gift of salvation was not given to you because of any works you had accomplished. That gift is granted solely by the grace of God. Scripture states that you are saved by God's grace and through your faith.

Yet, we well know that some gifts can be enjoyed for years to come. For example, if someone gave you a car or truck, that particular gift could last for five or more years. You could say that God's gift of salvation is the only gift that truly keeps on giving. This gift, when opened at salvation, will last for eternity and take years to fully appreciate.

Ephesians 2:10 states what God saved you for. First, you are "*His workmanship.*" This word originates from the Greek word *poiéma*, meaning "to make or do." (Please note that the primary language of the Old Testament was Hebrew, and the New Testament was Greek.) *Poiéma* refers to something made or created, emphasizing the craftsmanship or artistry involved in its creation. This word occurs only twice in all of the New Testament, here and in Romans 1:20.

In ancient Greek culture, the concept of *poiéma* was associated with artistic and literary works, highlighting the creator's skill and creativity. This term would have resonated with Jewish and Gentile audiences in the early Christian church because it conveyed the idea of intentional and purposeful creation.

The *New International Version* translates the term as *"we are God's handiwork."* The *New Living Translation* states that *"we are God's masterpiece."* Our English word "poem" is derived from *poiéma.*[4] Therefore, God is the divine Poet who is writing a masterpiece with His gift of your salvation.

In addition, Ephesians 2:10 (NKJV) explains that you were *"created in Christ Jesus for good works, which God prepared beforehand that we should walk in them."* Before you ever opened the gift of salvation, God had a plan and purpose for your life. His plan involves working through your life to produce good works. So, God created you to live out your salvation by doing good that would ultimately give Him glory.

You and I were not put on Earth to live out our plans for existence. Our Creator granted us life and gave us the gift of salvation so that we could enter a relationship with Him, so that He could write something extraordinary through our lives. His gift comes with His presence and power, enabling us to live out all He has planned for us.

So we were saved from the wages of our sin (death) and given a life God created that leads to good works. Thus, the gift of salvation opened on your spiritual birthday continually produces results throughout your life as you grow daily in your journey with Him.

Application:

Are you currently living out God's plan and purpose for your life? If not, how can you?

Prayer:

Lord, grant me a continual desire to become the masterpiece You are shaping through the life You have given me. I am blessed beyond measure to be able to live daily experiencing Your gift of grace…

Day 3

GOD LIVES IN YOU

Scripture Reading: 1 John 4:13–15

> *And God has given us his Spirit as proof that we live in him and he in us. Furthermore, we have seen with our own eyes and now testify that the Father sent his Son to be the Savior of the world. All who declare that Jesus is the Son of God have God living in them, and they live in God.*

Explanation:

Our God is omniscient, which means He has infinite awareness, understanding, and insight. Since God is all-knowing, He realizes we need assurance, guidance, and counsel. Our God is omnipotent, meaning He possesses unlimited power. Nothing is impossible with God because He can do anything. Our God is omnipresent, which means He is present in all places at all times. Our God knows we don't have the strength in and of ourselves to live the Christian life. Since He can be everywhere all the time, He places His power in our lives by inserting His Holy Spirit inside us the moment we are saved. We can't follow Jesus on our own strength. That is why the Holy Spirit resides within the heart of every believer.

Here is an illustration that may help you better understand this reality. What would happen if one of the greatest basketball players in the world, Steph Curry, took up residence inside you? What if he could empower you to have all of his basketball skills? What if his abilities to shoot and dribble a basketball were transferred to you? If you surrendered to Steph's ability within you, you would be granted abilities that far outweighed your own. On a basketball court, there would be nothing you couldn't accomplish.

While Steph Curry can't live inside you, the Holy Spirit of God can and does. God's power is available to you. God lives in and works through every believer who submits to His authority. Let that fact saturate your mind today. The incredible power of God indwells you. This means that nothing is impossible with you because nothing is impossible with God. The same power that raised Jesus from the dead lives inside every believer. (See Romans 8:11.) This means you never should say, "I can't," because Philippians 4:13 says, *"I can do all things through Christ who strengthens me"* (NKJV).

My illustration of Steph Curry has one major breakdown, though. God indwelling you doesn't mean you can do anything you want to. However, it does mean God will empower you to accomplish everything He calls you to do. That is incredible news! God will equip you and enable you to follow His will. Knowing that God lives in you should encourage you to follow Him wherever He leads.

The proof that we are His children is His Spirit, whom He has given us. (See 1 John 4:13.) His Spirit is proof *"that we live in him and he in us."* Then, verse 15 adds that Christians *"have God living in them, and they live in God."* There is a double residence that takes place in your life as a believer—God comes to live in you while, at the same time, you live in Him. You can't get a stronger union than a relationship with God, empowered by the Holy Spirit.

Application:

How do you know the Holy Spirit is within you? What does the Spirit of God enable you to do? How does His presence within you encourage you today?

Prayer:

God, I am so glad You didn't save me and leave me to live this life in my own strength. Instead, You placed Your Holy Spirit within me. I surrender to Your plan because I know You have all power...

Day 4

YOU CAN KNOW HIS LOVE

Scripture Reading: 1 John 4:16

> *We know how much God loves us, and we have put our trust in his love. God is love, and all who live in love live in God, and God lives in them.*

Explanation:

Today's verse is packed with profound truth concerning our relationship with God. We can know and experience God's love. In a world that is looking for love in all the wrong places, believers are loved by the *agape* love of God. *Agape* is the word for love found each time in 1 John 4:16. Below is an explanation of this kind of love:

> *Agapé* is a term used in the New Testament to describe a selfless, sacrificial, unconditional love. It is the highest form of love, often associated with the love of God for humanity and the love that believers are called to have for one another. Unlike other Greek words for love, such as "eros" (romantic love) or "philia" (brotherly love), *agapé* is not based on emotions or feelings but is an act of the will, characterized by a commitment to the well-being of others.[5]

God loves us unconditionally as an act of His will. Nobody can and will love you as much as Jesus does. What is even more amazing is the fact that you can know how much He loves you. The word for "know" in verse 16 is the Greek verb *ginóskó*. It describes knowledge gained through experience through a personal relationship. In the New Testament, it often denotes an intimate or relational knowledge, as opposed to mere intellectual understanding.[6] God doesn't want you simply to know about Him; He desires for you to have an intimate relationship with Him. God saves you into a relationship where you can understand His love for you on the deepest, most personal level.

Charles Swindoll shares another insight:

> This same Spirit who unites us to the life of God also unites us to the love of God, so that we're not only recipients of His love but also conduits of His love. (See 1 John 4:16.)
>
> In short, we're not left on our own to live up to the love of God in our own strength. In fact, that would be utterly impossible. We must never forget that in our flesh—our fallen condition with its sinful tendencies—we can't produce the kind of *agape* love that God manifests.[7]

We can intimately know His *agape* love and share that love with others. Through a growing relationship with Jesus, we progress in our understanding and knowledge of His love. The more we realize the nature of God's love, the greater we trust in Him.

Application:

In a world of people looking for love, how important is it to you to know God loves you? How can growing in the knowledge of His love help you build a stronger faith in God?

Prayer:

God, nobody can love me like You. I want to spend my life getting to know You more. Reveal Yourself to me daily and help me to understand the depths of Your love…

Day 5

HIS LOVE BUILDS CONFIDENCE

Scripture Reading: 1 John 4:17

> *And as we live in God, our love grows more perfect. So we will not be afraid on the day of judgment, but we can face him with confidence because we live like Jesus here in this world.*

Explanation:

As you deepen your relationship with Christ, He cultivates your love. The phrase *"grows more perfect"* in the New Testament language is the verb *teleioó*. This word conveys the idea of bringing something to its intended goal or state of completion. It often implies a process of maturing. *Teleioó* can refer to the fulfillment of a task, the completion of a journey, or the perfection of character.[8]

Like a runner completing a race by breaking the tape and crossing the finish line, God wants to bring your love to a state of completion. First John 4:13–17 shows the following progression:

- The more you realize God lives in you, the greater you understand His love.
- The greater your knowledge of His love, the more your love grows towards maturity.
- The more mature your love is in Christ, the greater confidence you can have as you approach a future judgment.

God does not want His children to be afraid on the day of judgment. Instead, He wants you to look forward to meeting Him with confidence. This verse reminds us that one day every person must give an account of their life. Judgment Day is coming for us all. Those who haven't trusted in Jesus Christ should be afraid of the judgment that awaits them. By refusing to accept the price Jesus paid for their sins, they will have to pay their own penalty. However, Christians have no fear of judgment because Jesus has paid for our sins at the cross. By accepting Christ as Savior, we have already received forgiveness of our sins.

I grew up viewing God as someone who couldn't wait to judge me. Some of the churches I attended taught so much about what a Christian shouldn't do that I was never really taught the benefits of being a believer. I later discovered that God didn't want me to live in fear of His judgment after I was saved. The exact opposite is true. God saved me so that I could know His love and live with confidence in my relationship with Him.

The word "confidence" actually means "all speech."[9] Imagine that you ran a red light that had a camera attached. Later, you received a ticket in the mail with a clear picture of your car running the light. If you attempted to take your case to court, nothing you said could override the truth found in the photograph. You would fear that appearance before the judge, because you know the truth.

In contrast, as a Christian, you can be assured of your salvation and know God loves you. Since you have a genuine relationship with Him, you can approach Judgment Day with complete confidence that God has forgiven your sins. Every word you speak can be spoken with the conviction that God loves you like He loves His Son.

Application:

Why does God want you to live with confidence rather than fear? What is your current level of confidence in Christ?

Prayer:

I love You, Lord, and I am so thankful that You saved me to a life that builds my confidence in my relationship with You. Please help my fears decrease and my assurance increase as I grow to know You more...

Day 6

HIS LOVE DRIVES OUT FEAR

Scripture Reading: 1 John 4:18

> *Such love has no fear, because perfect love expels all fear. If we are afraid, it is for fear of punishment, and this shows that we have not fully experienced his perfect love.*

Explanation:

There is some element of fear in every relationship outside of Jesus Christ. Even in great friendships and families, there is an underlying sense of fear because no one is perfect. We fear that our spouse will betray us, or our kids will make bad choices. When trust is lacking, worries and fears can linger in our minds. What if one of our family members comes down with cancer? We fear losing a spouse, parent, or child to death.

Have you ever considered that one massive difference between our bond with others and our relationship with Jesus is that we have no reason to fear? God will never leave or forsake us. (See Hebrews 13:5.) The Lord can be trusted entirely because He cannot lie. God makes good on every promise He makes. He is always present with us, so we have no reason to be afraid. He cannot die; thus, we don't have to fear ever losing Him. His love is perfect. Therefore, it never fails.

We never have to fear when we are loved by the God who created us and will one day judge the world. His love has no fear, because perfect love expels it. The word "expels" means "to throw." Just as God casts our sins as far as the East is from the West (see Psalm 103:12), He also throws fear away from our lives.

Believers can rest assured that they need not fear future judgment. If someone still struggles with fear in this area, it may be that they have not yet fully experienced the joy of salvation, or they may need a deeper understanding of God's complete forgiveness.

Scripture tells us what God does with Christians' sins upon their forgiveness. He places our sins behind His back (see Isaiah 38:17 NKJV) and remembers them no more. (See Hebrews 8:12.) Micah 7:19 declares that God throws our sins into the depths of the sea, to which the great missionary Corrie ten Boom added: "And put up a no fishing sign."[10]

When believers realize all that God has done with their sins, they have no reason to fear the judgment to come. If you are fully aware that you know God personally, you can have complete confidence that He loves you. God's perfect love produces the only relationship in your life where you never have to be afraid.

Application:

What are your thoughts on today's devotion? Why should these truths lead you to perfect peace in your relationship with Jesus?

Prayer:

Thank You, Jesus, for removing my fears of future judgment. Help me realize that Your love and forgiveness eliminate every reason to be afraid...

Day 7

GOD HAS A PURPOSE FOR YOU

Scripture Reading: John 10:10

> *The thief's purpose is to steal and kill and destroy. My purpose is to give them a rich and satisfying life.*

Explanation:

In each of the Gospels, Jesus clearly states why He came. His statements are as follows:

- *Don't be afraid of those who want to kill your body; they cannot touch your soul. Fear only God, who can destroy both soul and body in hell.* (Matthew 10:28)
- *For even the Son of Man came not to be served but to serve others and to give his life as a ransom for many.* (Mark 10:45)
- *For the Son of Man came to seek and save those who are lost.* (Luke 19:10)
- *The thief's purpose is to steal and kill and destroy. My purpose is to give them a rich and satisfying life.* (John 10:10)

In Matthew and Mark, Jesus emphasizes how He came to serve by His sacrificial death, which would pay the penalty for our sins. Luke highlights that God came looking for lost people to save them. Therefore, three out of Jesus's four purpose statements concern our salvation.

Yet, His purpose statement in John deals with the kind of life He came to give us. Jesus compares a shepherd in biblical times to Him being the Good Shepherd who takes care of His sheep. (See John 10:1–16.) Amid this comparison of a shepherd to the Good Shepherd, Jesus shares His purpose statement for leaving heaven and coming to Earth.

The *New King James Version* translates John 10:10 as *"The thief does not come except to steal, and to kill, and to destroy. I have come that they may have life, and that they may have it more abundantly."* The devil is the thief described in Jesus's analogy. The devil comes after the believer to steal, kill, and destroy. Satan's purpose is to take everything from you. Your ultimate enemy wants to kill anything that lives in your spiritual life. He desires to devastate your hope and demolish your dreams. However, Jesus comes to give you a rewarding and satisfying life. Christ's ultimate purpose is to bring you true fulfillment and unending joy.

Look at the last statement of the NKJV translation of John 10:10 and notice the comma. *"I have come that they may have life, and that they may have it more abundantly."* Now, consider these questions: Which side of the comma are you living on? Are you just living life and simply existing? Would you describe your daily experience as surviving or thriving? Are you experiencing the abundant life God has planned for you?

You see, God did not come to save you and watch you suffer until you reach heaven. Christ came to give you life more abundantly. He came to this Earth to defeat the devil. That means that Jesus doesn't want the devil to steal, kill, or destroy you. God has great plans for His children both now and forever.

Application:

How will you fulfill God's purpose for your life? In what specific ways can your spiritual life cause you to flourish rather than flounder? How does living with anything less than a satisfying life diminish Jesus's purpose for coming?

Prayer:

Jesus, I want to live in everything You came for. Help me to take hold of everything You purposed for me. I don't want to ever settle for anything less than Your best…

Part 2

FOLLOWING JESUS

The Bible records twenty-one times over twelve conversations where Jesus said, *"Follow me."* When Jesus spoke these words, He called His disciples and other followers to a more profound commitment and taught them about the cost and rewards of discipleship.

When Jesus verbalizes *"Follow Me,"* it is far more than a simple invitation to walk behind Him. While Bible study and biblical fellowship are vital to your walk, Jesus's call to follow Him goes way beyond those disciplines. Jesus calls us to follow Him because He knows a full commitment will lead to our complete transformation. At the heart of discipleship is following Jesus's call daily.

Following Jesus means prioritizing your relationship with Him, obeying His teaching, and embracing His values as your own. It signifies a willingness to deny ourselves, take up our cross daily, and commit to discipleship. To truly walk in His steps (see 1 Peter 2:21), we must stop making excuses and do whatever it takes to follow Jesus.

Follow along closely over this next week, as we examine what it takes to follow Jesus.

Day 8

"COME FOLLOW ME"

Scripture Reading: Matthew 4:18–22

> *One day as Jesus was walking along the shore of the Sea of Galilee, he saw two brothers—Simon, also called Peter, and Andrew—throwing a net into the water, for they fished for a living. Jesus called out to them, "Come, follow me, and I will show you how to fish for people!" And they left their nets at once and followed him. A little farther up the shore he saw two other brothers, James and John, sitting in a boat with their father, Zebedee, repairing their nets. And he called them to come, too. They immediately followed him, leaving the boat and their father behind.*

Explanation:

Today's text emphasizes God's call to His first disciples. The setting is *"the shore of the Sea of Galilee"* (v. 18). It is here that Jesus will call Peter, Andrew, James, and John. All four were fishermen whom Jesus invited to fish for men.

In verse 19, Jesus clarifies His call with a threefold proclamation followed by a threefold promise. The statement of His call is *"Come follow me."* This decree involved submission ("*Come*"), separation ("*Follow*"), and a focus on their Savior ("*Me*"). You must surrender your will to follow His will when He says, "*Come.*" You must separate from your comfort zone if you are going to successfully "*follow.*" If your focus doesn't remain on your Savior, you won't follow for long before returning to your old way of life.

This promise follows the proclamation: *"And I will show you how to fish for people!"* (v. 19). This promise depicts an image (*"fish for people"*). Jesus met these fishermen where they were. These four knew fishing, so they could relate to what Jesus promised them. Fishing involves patience, persistence, and proper skills. Fishing for men would require the same. When they felt the tug of their nets, excitement grew as they hauled in their catch. Likewise, seeing God work through them and witnessing others being saved would thrill their hearts and inspire them to keep fishing.

Second, Jesus promised His instruction (*"I will show you how."*) Jesus wouldn't call them to do something without teaching them how. Jesus will equip you for everything He commands you to do. Christ is the Master Teacher. If you faithfully follow Him as His disciple, you will definitely learn how to fish for people.

Yet, it won't be easy. Salvation is a free gift from God, but discipleship comes at a cost. Following Jesus will require dedication and discipline. The first disciples sacrificed to follow Christ. They left their boats and nets, which represented their identity and income. They obeyed Jesus's commands, so they surrendered their will to His. They submitted to being His disciples by committing to learn from Him. How can we, as His present-day disciples, expect any less commitment than His first disciples had in accepting Jesus's call to follow Him?

Application:

In what ways is God calling you out of your comfort zone to follow Him? How will you respond to His call to learn how to fish for people?

Prayer:

Jesus, help me to hear Your call in my heart daily: *"Come, follow Me, and I will show you how to fish for people!"* I need a daily reminder of how vital Your call is for my life...

Day 9

PRIORITIZING YOUR WALK

Scripture Reading: Luke 9:23 (NIV)

> *Then he said to them all: "Whoever wants to be my disciple..."*

Explanation:

Luke 9:23 is one of my life verses and life motto. A life verse is a Scripture that speaks personally to you in a special way. It is a passage that resonates intensely in your heart and inspires your life. I would challenge you to get an ink pad and put your fingerprint next to specific verses in God's Word that reverberate in your soul.

We will spend the next three days seeking God's truth from this one verse.

Like Matthew 4:19, this verse is a calling from God to His disciples. Jesus's declaration begins with a foundational principle for discipleship: If you are going to follow Jesus faithfully, you must consistently have a strong desire. Remember this: You will always have as much of Jesus in your life as you want. The problem is not God revealing Himself to you. His Word continually speaks to His revealing nature. He wants to be known by you. The difficulty in our relationship with Jesus always belongs to us, never to Him.

Meditate on the first part of Luke 9:23 from the following translations:

- *Then He said to them all, "If anyone desires to come after Me,..."* (NKJV)

- *Then he told them what they could expect for themselves: "Anyone who intends to come with me has to let me lead."* (MSG)

It starts with your desire and intentions. How much do you want to become a disciple of Jesus Christ? What level of commitment are you bringing to your relationship with Him?

Our prayers need to start with, "Lord help my want-to. Keep my desire strong for You."

You will need a stout dedication to Jesus if you intend to follow Jesus. The Christian life is not a sprint; it is a marathon. You will have high moments with your Savior, but there will also be times when you must walk through spiritual valleys. Your vow to Jesus cannot be based on your feelings, because a believer's journey is a walk by faith and not by sight. (See 2 Corinthians 5:7.)

Notice the progression from the prophet Isaiah:

> *But those who trust in the Lord will find new strength. They will soar high on wings like eagles. They will run and not grow weary. They will walk and not faint.*
>
> (Isaiah 40:31)

Did you catch the order of the verbs in verse 31? You would expect Isaiah to say that believers walk, then run, and finally soar with Jesus. However, the order is reversed: soar on wings like eagles, run and not grow weary, walk and not faint. Isaiah doesn't make the Christian life feel like an easy road. It is not. But it is worth every effort to follow Jesus. The key to consistency is in your daily walk with Christ. Sure, there will be soaring and running times, but it will often be your step-by-step following Jesus in a faithful walk where most of your spiritual growth will occur.

Application:

How much do you desire to follow Jesus? How can you stay faithful in your daily walk?

Prayer:

Jesus, I need You to keep my desire for You strong. Please, Lord, help me to hunger and thirst for righteousness continually...

Day 10

THE DISCIPLINE OF DENIAL

Scripture Reading: Luke 9:23 (NIV)

> *Then he said to them all: "Whoever wants to be my disciple must deny themselves."*

Explanation:

A significant aspect of wanting to follow Jesus depends on your ability to deny yourself. Self-denial is a vital spiritual discipline that takes years to develop. This is a good time to pause and clarify what I mean by a spiritual discipline. A spiritual discipline is a habit developed through faithful practice that leads to a stronger walk with Jesus. These disciplines include worship, prayer, Bible study, and self-denial. Each of the nine divisions in this book could be considered a spiritual discipline, and if practiced daily, could result in an incredible relationship with Jesus.

So, what do we mean by self-denial? *The Dictionary of Bible Themes* defines self-denial as "the willingness to deny oneself of possessions or status, to grow in holiness and commitment to God."[11] The idea of self-denial is revealed in Paul's words:

> *I once thought these things were valuable, but now I consider them worthless because of what Christ has done. Yes, everything else is worthless when compared with the infinite value of knowing Christ Jesus my Lord. For his sake I have discarded everything else, counting it all as*

> *garbage, so that I could gain Christ and become one with him.* (Philippians 3:7–9)

The key to self-denial is desiring God's will rather than your own selfish desires. This attitude is seen in the words of John the Baptist: *"He must become greater and greater, and I must become less and less"* (John 3:30).

Other aspects of self-denial are revealed in Paul's words to the believers in Galatia and Colossae:

> *Those who belong to Christ Jesus have nailed the passions and desires of their sinful nature to his cross and crucified them there. Since we are living by the Spirit, let us follow the Spirit's leading in every part of our lives. Let us not become conceited, or provoke one another, or be jealous of one another.* (Galatians 5:24–26)

> *Since you have been raised to new life with Christ, set your sights on the realities of heaven, where Christ sits in the place of honor at God's right hand. Think about the things of heaven, not the things of earth. For you died to this life, and your real life is hidden with Christ in God.* (Colossians 3:1–3)

Any inconsistency in your ability to deny self will cause major struggles in your journey with Jesus. While self-denial involves individual actions, it must become a way of life. No one act of denying yourself assures that you won't give in to your fleshly nature. That is why it is a spiritual discipline that must be consistently cultivated in your life.

Application:

What areas of your fleshy nature give you the most difficulty in denying yourself? How can you nurture your spiritual nature so that self-denial becomes a habit?

Prayer:

Holy Spirit, I do not have the strength to deny my selfish nature. I desperately need You to empower me to consistently say no to the things of this world and yes to You…

Day 11

TAKING UP YOUR CROSS DAILY

Scripture Reading: Luke 9:23 (NIV)

> *Then he said to them all: "Whoever wants to be my disciple must deny themselves and take up their cross daily and follow me."*

Explanation:

I hope you have noticed the sequence of Luke 9:23. Following Jesus begins with a desire, which requires self-denial, because you have a cross to take up daily.

What does Jesus mean when He says to take up our cross daily? R. C. Sproul gives a great explanation:

> Jesus is not talking about rigorous practices of asceticism whereby we deny ourselves a comfortable bed or three meals a day, although we may be called upon to do that from time to time, but he is talking about something beyond that. He is talking about a cross that is made for every Christian.
>
> There are few passages in the New Testament as misunderstood and abused as this particular passage. How many times have you heard people say, "I have a cross to bear," and that cross is the unemployment of the husband, or a debilitating illness, or an undisciplined child, and so on. The concept of bearing one's cross has become a way of describing any form of suffering that we are called upon to endure. But that is not what Jesus is referring to here. He is not referring to

> what we may call common forms of suffering, the kind that afflicts Christian and non-Christian alike, and has no bearing on a person's commitment to Christ. What Jesus is saying here is that when we take the name Christian, and openly identify ourselves with Christ, we must be ready not only to bear the normal suffering that life brings, but to share in the particular suffering of Christ.
>
> Unless we are willing to participate in the humiliation of Christ, we cannot participate in his exaltation.[12]

So, carrying your cross for Jesus does not mean wearing a cross necklace or a T-shirt. Crosses in Jesus's day were cruel places for humiliating deaths. There was nothing easy, beautiful, or pleasant about watching someone being crucified. Instead, crosses are ugly, messy, places of extreme sacrifice. Therefore, carrying your cross daily involves sacrificing your desires for God's plan and purpose.

If we aren't careful, we will mistake following Jesus for sitting on padded chairs in beautiful churches looking at Scripture on large video walls. While nothing is inherently wrong with these customs, following Jesus goes much deeper than church attendance. It involves sacrifice and suffering.

Some churches give invitations to follow Christ by appealing only to how it benefits the recipient. However, for early church followers and in many countries today, following Jesus involves a great sacrifice. That is because following Jesus is not first about us. It is all about Jesus Christ.

Application:

How can you deny yourself and take up your cross daily? What has it cost you to follow Jesus?

Prayer:

Jesus, You never promised that this life would be easy. But You did promise that You would never leave me nor forsake me. (See Hebrews 13:5.) Lord help my desire to follow You to be so strong that I will be willing to sacrifice whatever is needed to glorify You...

Day 12

COMMITMENT TO DISCIPLESHIP

Scripture Reading: Luke 9:24–26 (NIV)

> *For whoever wants to save their life will lose it, but whoever loses their life for me will save it. What good is it for someone to gain the whole world, and yet lose or forfeit their very self? Whoever is ashamed of me and my words, the Son of Man will be ashamed of them when he comes in his glory and in the glory of the Father and of the holy angels.*

Explanation:

Luke 9:24 introduces the problem and the paradox of the Christian life. Let's look first at the problem. As Jesus surrendered His life to the Father's will and died on the cross, so must His followers unselfishly live their lives for God. "*Whoever wants to save their life*" identifies people living for themselves. This attitude reflects a self-centered approach to life. People in this category strive to hold on to earthly rewards and temporary security. That is where the paradox enters. Those who live that way will one day lose all they tried to obtain. They focused on momentary external things you can't take with you when you die. So if you try to keep things that don't matter, you will eventually lose them.

However, Jesus said, "*whoever loses their life for me will save it.*" If you lose your selfish desires and live for Jesus, everything you focus on will last forever. Why is that true? Because everything done for God and His glory will last forever. The *Life Application Commentary on Luke* explains it as follows:

> That person will have given up in order to gain, and what is gained is of greater value indeed for it is eternal. Nothing that a person can possess or accomplish on this earth can compare with eternal life with Christ.
>
> The Greek word used here for "life" *(psuche)* means "self," referring to the whole person. Those who greedily grasp life, refusing to use it to help others, and focusing on satisfying their desires apart from God, will find that they have lost what they tried to keep. They lose eternal life and forfeit the spiritual fulfillment Christ can give. Those who invest their life for Christ and his kingdom will receive eternal life as well as the satisfaction of serving God on earth. Those who give up control to God find that he fills their lives with himself.[13]

Jesus then explains why you lose your life for Him to save it. *"What good is it for someone to gain the whole world, and yet lose or forfeit their very self?"* (Luke 9:25). *The Message* paraphrases it as follows: *"What good would it do to get everything you want and lose you, the real you?"* This is a great question that needs answering by how believers live their lives. Our lives are wasted if we aren't living for Jesus. That is our reason for living.

Those who are ashamed of Jesus will end up living for themselves. Christians who are willing to stand up for Jesus care more about what Jesus thinks than how the world responds. Living for Jesus and eternal rewards involves a sincere commitment to discipleship.

Application:

How can self-centeredness cause you to miss out on everything that matters?

Prayer:

You are my perfect example, Jesus, of losing your life so I could be saved. I need You to crucify anything in my selfish nature and help me to live unashamed for You...

Day 13

NO EXCUSES

Scripture Reading: Luke 9:57–62 (NIV)

> *As they were walking along the road, a man said to him, "I will follow you wherever you go." Jesus replied, "Foxes have dens and birds have nests, but the Son of Man has no place to lay his head." He said to another man, "Follow me." But he replied, "Lord, first let me go and bury my father." Jesus said to him, "Let the dead bury their own dead, but you go and proclaim the kingdom of God." Still another said, "I will follow you, Lord; but first let me go back and say goodbye to my family." Jesus replied, "No one who puts a hand to the plow and looks back is fit for service in the kingdom of God."*

Explanation:

Jesus called many people to follow Him, yet few accepted the call. Some made great boasts about following Him, but gave excuses when Jesus revealed the hardships of discipleship. Three people in today's Scripture claimed they would follow Jesus, but none of them actually did. The first wouldn't follow Jesus because he would have to leave the comfort of his house and travel. Two other men prioritized their family and said goodbye to them over following Jesus. It is amazing how many excuses we can make to the Lord when we're not fully committed to Him.

I researched the top excuses believers use for not doing what God has called us to do. Here is what I discovered:

1. "I can't."

2. "I don't know how."
3. "I don't have time."
4. "I'm all alone."
5. "I'm afraid."
6. "I can't afford it."[14]

Because of these excuses, many people won't do what God commands. Additionally, I came across a list of reasons why Christians claim they don't witness.

1. "I don't know how."
2. "I'm afraid of rejection."
3. "It's not my job."
4. "Evangelism is awkward."
5. "I'm not ready for hard questions."
6. "My life doesn't match my message."
7. "Christianity has a stigma."
8. "I don't know how to bring it up naturally."
9. "It doesn't seem that important."
10. "I don't want to be made fun of."[15]

What is amazing is that nobody would use any of these excuses for not striving to be the best they can be at their occupation. People would rise to the task if they had to speak up, risk awkward moments, and be rejected in order to make a significant income.

The truth may be too hard to swallow. Perhaps we prioritize worldly things over following the One who created the world! If we loved Jesus with all our hearts, souls, minds, and strength (see Mark 12:30–31), could we eliminate all our flimsy excuses?

Application:

How will people overcome these same excuses to make more money, play a sport, or start a hobby? What does this say about where Jesus is on their priority list?

Prayer:

You sacrificed so much for me, Lord. You went to the cross and died without making excuses. Please, Lord, help me not to miss out on living daily for You because of weak justifications. Instead, make me strong in faith so that I will follow You no matter what may come my way...

Day 14

IN HIS STEPS

Scripture Reading: 1 Peter 2:21 (NIV)

> *To this you were called, because Christ suffered for you, leaving you an example, that you should follow in his steps.*

Explanation:

Most people have heard of the phrase "What Would Jesus Do?" Maybe you grew up wearing the W.W.J.D. bracelets or T-shirts. What you might not know is that this question was posed by Charles Sheldon back in 1897. Over 125 years ago, Sheldon asked this question in his classic book, *In His Steps*. Sheldon's book examines what the world would be like if everyone paused to ask the question "What Would Jesus Do?" before they went about their daily lives. Sheldon pictured what life would look like if everyone sought to follow the steps that Jesus might take if He faced a similar situation.

In His Steps contains a story about a small American town called Raymond, where members of the snobbish First Church undertake a revolutionary pledge of "What Would Jesus Do?" that transforms their understanding of Christianity. Under the leadership of their pastor, Henry Maxwell, the lives of some of the most prominent members of Raymond are turned upside down as they seek to follow in the steps of Jesus.

Sheldon wrote the following in his bestselling book:

> The greatest question in all of human life is summed up when we ask, "What would Jesus do?" if, as we

> ask it, we also of Jesus Himself. We must know Jesus before we can imitate Him.[16]

Charles Sheldon based *In His Steps* on 1 Peter 2:21. Peter writes, "*To this you were called...*" Peter is referring to his discussion that began in 1 Peter 2:13–18. He had been speaking directly to people who were suffering as slaves. He goes on to say, "***because Christ suffered for you...***" We have a Savior who knows suffering.

Peter then writes: "*leaving you an example...*" The Greek word for "example" is *hypogrammos*. This word comes from *hypos*, which means "under" and *grammos*, which means "something written." In biblical times, the word was used to describe a pattern of letters children would use to learn to write. They would put the patterns of letters under what they were writing on, copy over them, and learn to write. Jesus is the pattern by which all believers learn.[17]

First Peter 2:21 closes with another metaphor of imitating Christ: "*that you should follow in His steps.*" Striving to follow Jesus doesn't mean we will walk the same road He walked. Only Christ could go to the cross and achieve salvation for all mankind. Instead, it means that we are to walk in a comparable way with a similar posture. Doing this would lead to a more faithful life and a growing relationship with Him.[18]

Application:

How impactful would it be if you paused daily to ask, "What would Jesus do?" in every decision you faced? How can you strategically walk in the steps of Jesus? In other words, how can you imitate Jesus's example?

Prayer:

Jesus, I need Your help to follow in Your steps. I can't follow You without the Holy Spirit's power, and if I don't know

Your heart. Help me to study Scripture daily to make me more aware of how You dealt with different situations, and please give me wisdom and discernment...

Part 3

FINDING GOD'S WILL

To obey God's will, you must know His will. To know His will, you must study His Word and seek His guidance. R. C. Sproul writes:

> God delights to hear the prayers of His people when they individually ask, "Lord, what do you want me to do?" The Christian pursues God, looking for His marching orders, seeking to know what course of action is pleasing to Him. This search for the will of God is a holy quest—a pursuit that is to be undertaken with vigor by the godly person.[19]

One of the significant issues in modern Christianity is the intense focus many believers have on God's hidden, mysterious will for their personal lives, while neglecting His revealed will for all believers as found in Scripture. We tend to start vigorously searching for God to show us His specific will before we look at His general will for all Christians. Therefore, the first question is not, "What is God's will for my life?" but "What is God's will?" His specific will for you will emerge from His general will for all Christians.

Over the next seven days, we will examine what Scripture plainly says is God's will for every follower of Jesus Christ.

Day 15

HIS WILL FOR ALL BELIEVERS

Scripture Reading: Proverbs 3:5–6

> *Trust in the Lord with all your heart; do not depend on your own understanding. Seek his will in all you do, and he will show you which path to take.*

Explanation:

Finding God's will begins with trusting the Lord with all your heart. Raymond C. Ortlund illustrates and explains the essence of wholeheartedly trusting God:

> A man crossed the Susquehanna River on a winter day. He did not know how thick the ice was. So he crawled along on all fours, gingerly feeling his way forward, when he heard some racket and clatter coming up behind him. He looked back, saw a wagon pulled by four horses, and noticed the driver whipping them along at a pretty good clip across the frozen river. The guy was a local man, so he knew how thick the ice was.
>
> Too many Christians are like the man down on all fours, creeping along, way too cautious. Their trust in the Lord is halfhearted. Then along comes a wholehearted Christian, and he changes the tone for everyone around.
>
> This Hebrew verb, translated as "trust," means to lie down in complete reliance. It pictures someone who stakes everything on God's promises.

> You can put your full weight down on Jesus Christ. He will never fail anyone who trusts Him radically. He is real. He is all He claims to be. He is right now all He has ever been to anyone anywhere. And He offers His total Self to you today on terms of total grace. What He deserves and demands is your total trust in the love, mercy, and wisdom of God in Christ alone.[20]

The main hindrance to total trust in Jesus is the temptation to *"lean...on your own understanding"* (NKJV). Ortlund clarifies the second phrase in Proverbs 3:5.

> Do you merely agree with the Bible, or do you obey the Bible? What do you do when the Bible contradicts what you want to be true? If you are looking in the Bible for excuses to do what you want anyway, you have, in fact, rejected God. But if you trust the Lord, you will let the Bible challenge your most cherished thoughts and feelings. He wants to speak into your life in ways that will help you. If you trust him wholeheartedly, you will let him teach you.[21]

Finding God's will involves trusting God rather than depending on your understanding. We must take God at His Word and follow His will regardless of what He calls us to do. As He contemplated the cross, Jesus's words in the Garden of Gethsemane provide the perfect example: *"Father, if you are willing, take this cup from me; yet not my will, but yours be done"* (Luke 22:42 NIV). God's will for every believer starts with surrendering to His Word.

Application:

Are you willing to obey God's Word no matter how you feel?

Prayer:

Lord, help me to follow Your will rather than my own. I know You know best for this life You have given me. I don't want to miss Your perfect will because I wouldn't surrender my desires to You…

Day 16

THE GREATEST COMMANDMENT

Scripture Reading: Matthew 22:36–40

> *"Teacher, which is the most important commandment in the law of Moses?" Jesus replied, "'You must love the* LORD *your God with all your heart, all your soul, and all your mind.' This is the first and greatest commandment. A second is equally important: 'Love your neighbor as yourself.' The entire law and all the demands of the prophets are based on these two commandments."*

Explanation:

An expert lawyer tested Jesus, inquiring which commandment was the most important. At the time of this question, Pharisees had identified over six hundred laws. They had often debated over which ones held the most significance. Some religious experts attempted to categorize the laws into major and minor groups. They were highly legalistic, while also extremely hypocritical. They considered the laws they obeyed as "more important," while they ignored the ones they labeled as "less important." This approach allowed them to condemn others without convicting themselves.

First, Jesus told them the first commandment was to love God. The priority of the Christian life is loving Jesus with your entire being—heart, soul, and mind. Jesus's answer highlighted the Pharisees' misplaced priorities. They cared more about keeping the law than loving God. What good is obeying God out of religion if you are not truly in love with Him? Jesus wants a relationship, and anything we do for Him should be motivated by the fact that we love Him. The Pharisees had wrong motives for following the rules, and the first part of Jesus's reply shifted everything back to love.

Second, when asked about the most excellent command, Jesus gave two commandments. In doing so, Christ connected our love for God to how we love others. The Pharisees were not in love with God and showed no love whatsoever to others. According to Jesus, the greatest commandment is twofold: the extent of someone's love for God is directly connected to how much they love others.

Jesus adds, "*The entire law and all the demands of the prophets are based on these two commandments*" (Matthew 22:40). Each one of the over 600 laws is founded on a person's love for God and others. You obey all of God's laws because you have a strong love for Him, which overflows to others. You don't keep God's laws out of obligation, but out of love.

Interestingly, the question originally meant to test Jesus helps us know if we pass the most basic test of following God's will. In other words, how can you ever say you follow God's desires for your life if you fail to obey the greatest commandment that all other commandments are based upon?

Finding God's will results from a love relationship with Him. How can anyone expect to find God's specific will for their life if they disobey His greatest commandment for all believers, clearly stated in His Word?

Application:

How is your love for God attached to your love for others? How are they both connected to finding His will?

Prayer:

Lord, help my love for You to grow stronger each day, so that I can love others as I should. I want to know Your will because I am convinced that You love me and have good plans in store…

Day 17

LIVING A HOLY LIFE

Scripture Reading: 1 Thessalonians 4:3

> *God's will is for you to be holy, so stay away from all sexual sin.*

Explanation:

God has a stated will, which means He clearly details through Scripture what He expects of all believers. In Paul's first letter to the Christians at Thessalonica, he clearly states that God's plan is for every believer to be holy.

There are two significant words found in today's verse. The first word is "*will.*" The New Testament word is *thélēma*, which means "to desire or wish," and it is often used in Scripture to refer to God's preferred will. In other words, this is God's best offer to people, which can be accepted or rejected.[22]

This means that God's will is for every Christian to be holy. That is His "Plan A" for all of us. However, God allows you free will to choose to follow His plan for your life. So, there is a permissive will where God permits you to live in less than His best if you follow your will instead of His. Many Christians live with far less power and peace than God desires for their lives. Why live in your "Plan B through Z," when God has a Plan A for your life?

The second word is "holy," which is the Greek word *hagiasmós*. This word refers to the process of becoming holy and set apart. It is used to describe sanctification, the process of progressing in holiness. *Hagiasmós* describes a believer being progressively transformed by the Lord into His likeness.[23]

Tom Wright helps us understand what God means when He says you are to be holy:

> For Paul, the word "holiness" draws its strength from the circle of ideas that belonged with the Temple in Jerusalem. If you went there to be in God's presence, holiness was mandatory. Special purification rituals were prescribed. It was vital that you come before the living God, the ultimately and utterly holy one, in a state of complete purity. They must therefore be as holy in all the details of their lives as if they were constantly in the Temple in Jerusalem.[24]

God has called us to a life of holiness and moral purity. He empowers us and calls us to live a life set apart for His glory. This doesn't mean we can be sinless because we still live with a fleshly body. However, God does give us victory over our temptations, and every believer should be growing in holiness.

Paul says, "*Stay away from sexual sins*" (1 Thessalonians 4:3), which refers to moral purity. Scripture is clear that the body is the temple of the Holy Spirit. (See 1 Corinthians 3:17; 6:19.) Therefore, as believers, our bodies house the Holy Spirit of God. This means that God desires us to conduct ourselves with holiness in our personal relationships.

Application:

What are your thoughts on the following quote by Ben Witherington regarding moral purity? "There are thus two aspects to sanctification, divine initiative and human endeavor."[25]

Prayer:

Jesus, I know Your will is for me to live set apart for Your glory. I also recognize that Your power is always available to help me follow Your will. Help me to strive for holiness…

Day 18

REJOICE ALWAYS

Scripture Reading: 1 Thessalonians 5:16, 18 (NIV)

> *Rejoice always,…for this is God's will for you in Christ Jesus.*

Explanation:

Yesterday, we studied Paul's words found in 1 Thessalonians 4:3 that clarified God's will for us to live holy lives in the area of sexual purity. Today, we begin a three-day journey through Paul's words, one chapter later from the same letter. In three verses (1 Thessalonians 5:16–18), Paul gives us three succinct phrases that are God's will for us in Christ Jesus. The first one is found in verse 16, "*rejoice always.*"

If I were to ask which Bible verse is the shortest, many would point to John 11:35, "*Jesus wept.*" However, that's not the shortest verse. The shortest verse in the Bible is 1 Thessalonians 5:16: "*Rejoice always.*" You might think they are equally short since both contain two words. Here's a tip for winning your next Bible trivia game: John 11:35 is three words in the Greek New Testament. Meanwhile, 1 Thessalonians 5:16 consists of only two words: "always rejoice." The Greek word *Pantote* means "always," and *Chairo* translates to "to delight in God's grace." Therefore, in Greek, the shortest verse is indeed "*Rejoice always.*"[26]

This verse reflects God's will for you—to "*rejoice always.*" But what does that entail? In all three phrases, the verbs used are in the present tense, meant to convey continual action. Rightly translated, it means: "Be continually rejoicing. Be continually praying. Be continually giving thanks." In addition, they are all plural, indicating that they are instructions for all believers, not just a select few. Rejoice collectively, pray collectively, and give thanks collectively. Also, all three verbs are commands, not suggestions—God isn't saying to be joyful only when it's convenient, but as a constant reality. We must consciously choose to obey these commands.[27]

Is it feasible to always rejoice? Can we maintain joy in every situation, during struggles as well as triumphs? Absolutely! God wouldn't command us to *"rejoice always"* without equipping us to do so. However, we must note that there is a significant difference between joy and happiness. Joy is an internal state, while happiness is an external experience. Joy comes from within, but happiness depends on circumstances. While happiness can fluctuate based on life events, joy stems from the presence of Christ within you.

As you grow in your walk with Christ, never forget that God's preferred will is that you experience the joy of Jesus throughout any and every circumstance of life. You can choose joy when you face trials of any kind (see James 1:2), because continual joy is God's will for your life.

Application:

How would you define joy? How can you experience joy continually?

Prayer:

Lord, please help me to choose joy no matter what difficulties come my way. I know it is Your will for me to consistently experience inner delight because You saved me to live an abundant life. (See John 10.) Please give me the strength to follow Your will...

Day 19

PRAY WITHOUT CEASING

Scripture Reading: 1 Thessalonians 5:17, 18 (NIV)

> *Pray continually,…for this is God's will for you in Christ Jesus.*

Explanation:

In verse 17, God gives another command that is His will for every Christian: "*pray continually.*" Remember that this is a present-tense, plural imperative. God knows how critically important it is for His followers to stay in constant communication with Him. That is why He commands it, because He wants us to remain in His will.

We will talk more about the spiritual discipline of prayer later (Days 22–32), but for now, we just need to know that continual prayer is His will for our lives. Yet, we must clarify the difference between "saying prayers" and "praying prayers." God isn't interested in us "saying prayers." In other words, He doesn't want us reciting prayers from memory, void of our hearts connecting with Him. Prayers like "Now I lay me down to sleep, I pray the Lord my soul to keep," are cute for young children, but they aren't quite the depths of communication. While prayers at mealtime or bedtime are meaningful, God also desires His children to mature in their prayer life to deepen their relationship with Him. We need to pray our prayers.

Interestingly, the word for "pray" in this verse is the Greek word *proseúxomai,* which consists of two words that literally mean "moving towards exchanging wishes." It can also be translated as "interacting with the Lord by switching our wishes for His desires, and He imparts faith into our lives."[28] Therefore, this word for pray is closely connected with our faith in Him. Praying prayers means sharing our hearts with Jesus and submitting to His will.

Obviously, praying without ceasing means something other than constantly saying prayers, or the command is impossible. J. B. Lightfoot once said that prayer consists not "in the moving of the lips, but the elevation of the heart to God."[29]

Having distinguished between reciting prayers and praying from the heart, we must delve deeper into the concept of unceasing prayer. To pray without ceasing means that prayer becomes the entirety of the Christian life, not merely a part of it. Continuously praying is not the goal for a few spiritual elites but is the attainable reality for every Christ-follower. As we noted yesterday, with God's command to always rejoice, our Lord would never command us to do something impossible.

John Wesley explained the command to pray without ceasing as follows:

> Whether we think of, or speak to, God, whether we act or suffer for Him, all is prayer when we have no other object than His love, and the desire of pleasing Him.
>
> Prayer continues in the desire of the heart. In souls filled with love, the desire to please God is a continual prayer.[30]

Application:

How does the following statement by Warren Wiersbe connect to today's devotion?

"We are to keep the receiver off the hook and be in touch with God so that our praying is part of a long conversation that is never broken."[31]

Prayer:

Jesus, my Savior, help my thoughts and words to be in tune with Your will for my life at all times. I realize that my faith is connected to my desire to stay in constant communication with You...

Day 20

GIVE THANKS IN ALL CIRCUMSTANCES

Scripture Reading: 1 Thessalonians 5:18 (NIV)

> *Give thanks in all circumstances; for this is God's will for you in Christ Jesus.*

Explanation:

God gives yet another command, which is His will for all believers: "*Give thanks in all circumstances.*" Someone might wonder, "How can I give thanks in every circumstance?" Let me ask you: Do you believe that He allows everything you experience for His glory and your benefit?

If you trust that everything is filtered through Him for His glory and your welfare—and that "*all things work together for good for those who love God*" (Romans 8:28 NET)—expressing gratitude to God in all circumstances should come instinctively!

Paul told Christians at Philippi to: "*Always be full of joy in the Lord. I say it again—rejoice!*" (Philippians 4:4). When Paul emphasizes the command to rejoice twice in Philippians 4:4, it suggests that the situation in Philippi made rejoicing seem unreasonable. Despite the circumstances, whether problems or persecution, Paul insists on a joyous attitude of gratitude. This message was a central theme throughout the apostle Paul's life.

Gratitude is a choice you make because of who God is and what He has done.

First, we should be grateful for who God is. God is characterized by love, joy, peace, holiness, kindness, and faithfulness. As God's children, we are to reflect His attributes.

Second, we should be thankful for what God has done. Note the following verses of Scripture:

> *But God shows his love for us in that while we were still sinners, Christ died for us.* (Romans 5:8 ESV)
>
> *Nevertheless, do not rejoice in this, that the spirits are subject to you, but rejoice that your names are written in heaven.* (Luke 10:20 ESV)

God sent Jesus to die for us so that our sins could be forgiven and our names written in the Lamb's Book of Life. If God never did anything else besides provide for our salvation, we should be continually thankful. Yet, on top of salvation, God continually blesses us with what we need to live a spiritually abundant life.

The key to obeying the commands in 1 Thessalonians 5:16–18 is the last phrase, "*in Christ Jesus.*" You have the power to obey all of God's commands supernaturally! When you were born again (saved), God put the Holy Spirit in your life to empower you to obey His commands. When you embrace God's great purpose and power for you, it profoundly changes how you act and relate to others, manifesting noticeable and significant growth in your spiritual journey.

Application:

How can you choose gratitude as an ongoing attitude?

Prayer:

God, thank You for sending Jesus to save me from my sins and for sending the Holy Spirit to empower me to obey Your commands. I choose to have an attitude of gratitude today and always…

Day 21

HIS SPECIFIC WILL FOR YOU

Scripture Reading: James 1:5

> *If you need wisdom, ask our generous God, and he will give it to you. He will not rebuke you for asking.*

Explanation:

Over the last few days, we have discovered that God has a general will for every believer. For instance, He desires for us to love Him and others, pursue purity, rejoice always, pray without ceasing, and give thanks in all circumstances. These are a few of God's purposes found in His Word.

Scripture also teaches us that God wants us to know His specific will for every individual believer. While God doesn't always show us everything up front, He will reveal His purpose in a timely manner as we grow in our daily walk. However, make no mistake about it: God wants you to seek His will so that you can know His plans for your unique life.

James, the half-brother of Jesus, stated in one word how you can discover God's will: "*Ask.*" When you need wisdom and discernment to discover God's will, ask the One who knows. God created your life and has a specific purpose for it. As you seek His will, pray, asking Him to disclose it to you. James characterizes God as "*generous*" because not only does He have all the resources, but He is a lavish giver.

Read carefully the following Scriptures and notice how they coincide with today's verse:

> *This is the confidence we have in approaching God: that if we ask anything according to his will, he hears us. And if we know that he hears us—whatever we ask—we know that we have what we asked of him.*
>
> (1 John 5:14–15 NIV)

> *You don't have what you want because you don't ask God for it. And even when you ask, you don't get it because your motives are all wrong—you want only what will give you pleasure.* (James 4:2–3)

You can have confidence asking God what His will is for your life. He always hears your prayers, and His unchanging desire is that you know and follow His will. There are only three possible reasons a believer doesn't know God's will:

1. It is not yet time for God to reveal His will.
2. You haven't asked.
3. You have asked with the wrong motives.

Therefore, if the timing is correct and you ask with the right motive, you can rest assured that God will answer your prayer concerning His will for your life. Just ask and keep on asking!

Application:

How much confidence and motivation does it give you to know that God wants to reveal His will to you? Why do you believe some Christians fail to ask God for wisdom to know His will?

Prayer:

I pray the following over you today from Hebrews 13:20–21 (NIV). Make it your daily prayer for yourself and others:

Now may the God of peace, who through the blood of the eternal covenant brought back from the dead our Lord Jesus, that great Shepherd of the sheep, equip you with everything good for doing his will, and may he work in us what is pleasing to him, through Jesus Christ, to whom be glory for ever and ever. Amen.

Part 4

THE PRIORITY OF PRAYER

Jesus placed a high priority on prayer. Scripture records that He often set aside private time to talk to His Father. Luke 5:16 reads: *"But Jesus often withdrew to the wilderness for prayer."* As you study Scripture, you will notice how often He prayed. Here are just a few times Scripture records Jesus praying:

- At His baptism (see Luke 3:21–22)
- Before choosing His disciples (see Luke 6:12–13)
- While speaking to the Jewish leaders (see Matthew 11:25–26)
- Before feeding the 5,000 (see John 6:11)
- Before feeding the 4,000 (see Mark 15:36)
- Before walking on water (see Matthew 14:23)
- While healing a deaf and mute man (see Mark 7:31–37)
- At the Transfiguration (see Luke 9:28–29)
- At the return of the seventy-two (see Luke 10:21)
- Before raising Lazarus from the dead (see John 11:41–42)
- At the Lord's Supper (see Matthew 26:26)
- In Gethsemane, before His betrayal (see Matthew 26:36–46)
- While dying on the cross (see Matthew 27:46)

Scripture proves that Jesus prioritized praying to the Father. If Jesus needed to spend quality and quantity time conversing with His Father, His followers must also prioritize prayer. Over the next eleven days, we will examine how essential prayer is to your journey with Jesus.

Day 22

COMMUNICATION IS KEY

Scripture Reading: Mark 1:35 (NIV)

> *Very early in the morning, while it was still dark, Jesus got up, left the house and went off to a solitary place, where he prayed.*

Explanation:

Jesus gives us an incredible example to follow. Jesus made prayer a priority even though He was always extremely busy. He intentionally got up early, went to a quiet place, and spent undistracted time with God. He knew how vital communication with Father God was to His life and mission on Earth.

No relationship can thrive without ongoing, honest communication. Therefore, your prayer life is foundational to your connection with God. I don't know one believer who doesn't recognize their need for a strong prayer life. Yet, many Christians admit that their prayer life is sporadic. In addition, many struggle with how to speak with the God who spoke the universe into existence.

We need to realize how much God desires a relationship with us and how much we need daily time with Jesus for guidance, hope, encouragement, and spiritual growth. The only way to know God better is through regular time spent with Him.

Jesus is your Savior, Lord, Shepherd, Counselor, and Friend. In John 15:15, Jesus made this statement to His first disciples:

> *I no longer call you slaves, because a master doesn't confide in his slaves. Now you are my friends, since I have told you everything the Father told me.*

Your prayer life with Jesus is the most intimate relationship you will ever experience, because nobody knows you like Jesus. Remember when you pray to Him, He already knows everything about you. He knows your thoughts, fears, struggles, and sins. So, Christ desires that you speak to Him with an open and honest heart.

Remember that Jesus is full of grace and truth. (See John 1:14 NIV.) You can always trust Him to be honest. He extends forgiveness, and His love never fails. God doesn't want a formal exchange where you think to yourself how things sound to Him before you speak. He wants you to share your heart.

Prioritizing prayer and integrating it into your daily life can lead to significant spiritual growth. You grow to know God personally when you treat prayer as an essential part of your day rather than just an obligation or a last resort. By practicing prayer consistently, you establish an ongoing dialogue with God, fostering a relationship that positively influences every aspect of your life.

Application:

Pastor Chris Hodges gave a profound question concerning the priority of prayer:

> Think for a moment: How would your life be different if you were to pray first before everything you do?[32]

Prayer:

Lord, I know I need to prioritize my time in prayer with You. I commit today to spend more time in prayer with You because You are, by far, the most important relationship in my life...

Day 23

PRAYER IS A DIALOGUE

Scripture Reading: Psalm 17:6

> *I am praying to you because I know you will answer, O God. Bend down and listen as I pray.*

Explanation:

Many of us are prone to approach prayer as a monologue. In other words, we only pray when we need something from God. We might have a daily prayer time of five minutes a day, where we give God our prayer list. How would you feel as a parent if your children only spoke to you when they needed something from you? You would feel as if your children didn't love you and that they just used you! If we are not careful, we could treat our heavenly Father the same way. God wants us to speak with Him because we love Him, not just because we need something. Sometimes we pray for everything we think we need and forget that a relationship with Him is all that matters.

Others approach prayer by sitting for hours and meditating. Some clear their minds, waiting for God to say something. They sit before Him, but they never share with Him. They think a relationship with God can only be found through a certain posture or practice.

However, prayer was meant to be a dialogue, not a monologue. Prayer is both speaking and listening. That's how a relationship works. Billy Graham said it best when he said, "Prayer is simply a two-way conversation between you and God."[33] Charles Stanley calls prayer, "The Ultimate Conversation."[34]

In Psalm 17:6, David twice suggests the dialogue of prayer. He states, "*I am praying to you because I know you will answer.*" David knew that if he spoke honestly to God, he would receive a reply. Then, David pleads with God to "*Bend down and listen as I pray.*" This is a beautiful picture of what happens through a dialogue involving participants speaking and listening. David believed that his God on high would stoop down and attentively listen as He cried out to Him in prayer.

Notice the dialogue of prayer revealed in these Scriptures:

> *I took my troubles to the Lord; I cried out to him, and he answered my prayer.* (Psalm 120:1)
>
> *Ask me and I will tell you remarkable secrets you do not know about things to come.* (Jeremiah 33:3)
>
> *I am the good shepherd; I know my own sheep, and they know me, just as my Father knows me and I know the Father. So I sacrifice my life for the sheep...My sheep listen to my voice; I know them, and they follow me.* (John 10:14–15, 27)

Prayer was always intended to be a conversation between you and God. Only when you learn to speak and listen do you open up unlimited potential in your prayer life.

Application:

In what ways is your prayer time with God a dialogue?

Do you spend more time talking than listening? What areas need improvement in your communication with God?

Prayer:

I am amazed that You would take the time to bend down and listen to my words. I need to spend more time listening to You. Speak to me clearly, Lord, Your servant and friend is listening...

Day 24

ASK. SEEK. KNOCK.

Scripture Reading: Matthew 7:7–8

> *Keep on asking, and you will receive what you ask for. Keep on seeking, and you will find. Keep on knocking, and the door will be opened to you. For everyone who asks, receives. Everyone who seeks, finds. And to everyone who knocks, the door will be opened.*

Explanation:

Matthew 7:7–11 occurs towards the end of Jesus's famous Sermon on the Mount. This was the greatest sermon ever preached by the greatest preacher who ever lived—Jesus. During this sermon, Jesus taught the Beatitudes or "the attitudes that ought to be" in a Christian's life. Then Jesus continued in Matthew 6 and 7 to give some challenging and pointed teachings about how believers should live out their Christian lives.

Bruce Barton shares the following explanation of today's Scripture:

> Beginning in chapter 5, the Sermon on the Mount has thus far explained to Jesus's followers the lifestyle and life attitudes that he expected from them. Some may have heard and thought the demands to be impossible. Here, Jesus gave the answer to those thoughts and questions—*ask, seek, knock*. The ability to live for God is only a prayer away. The verbs are in the present tense, indicating continuous activity. Jesus's followers

> can keep on asking, keep on seeking, and keep on knocking, indicating the importance of persistent, consistent prayer in their lives. Only through prayer can believers stay in contact with God, know what he wants them to do, and then have the strength to do God's will in all areas of life. God will answer believers who persistently ask, seek, and knock. Jesus promised, *"For everyone who asks receives, and everyone who searches finds, and for everyone who knocks, the door will be opened."* God had told the prophet Jeremiah, *"You will seek Me and find Me when you seek Me with all your heart"* (Jeremiah 29:13). The three words (ask, seek, knock) combine to emphasize the truth that those who bring their needs to God can trust that they will be satisfied. All three are metaphors for praying. Sometimes God does not answer our prayers immediately; sometimes we must keep on knocking, awaiting God's answer. However, if we continue to trust God through prayer, Jesus promised that we will receive, find, and have an open door.
>
> Knowing God takes faith, focus, and follow-through, and Jesus assures us that we will be rewarded. Don't give up in your efforts to seek God, even when the doors seem closed. Continue to ask him for more knowledge, patience, wisdom, love, and understanding. He will give them to you.[35]

The only way to pray persistently is to pray continually. It is through faithful prayer that we grow to trust God more.

Application:

How persistent are you in asking, seeking, and knocking? What keeps you from being more persistent?

Prayer:

Please give me the strength to keep asking, seeking, and knocking. I know that You, Lord, love me and that You are a God who answers prayers…

Day 25

LEARNING TO PRAY

Scripture Reading: Luke 11:1–2

> *Once Jesus was in a certain place praying. As he finished, one of his disciples came to him and said, "Lord, teach us to pray, just as John taught his disciples." Jesus said, "This is how you should pray."*

Explanation:

Spiritual disciplines are like physical disciplines, such as working out. You only increase in strength the more you lift weights and exercise. The more you pray, the better you become as a communicator and listener. The disciples had witnessed Jesus's praying, so one asked Jesus to teach them how to pray. They were awed by the way Jesus prayed and knew His connection with the Father, and they wanted to achieve that level in their own prayer life. Prayer is something you must learn to do. If His first disciples needed to learn how, so does every follower of Christ.

Charles Swindoll shares a personal illustration that relates to how most people approach prayer. He shares how he attempted to put together a Christmas present without reading the instructions. After making a mess of things, he finally grabbed the instructions.

> Humbled and teachable, I started reading from the top of the page where, to my dismay, a sarcastic sage had written in very small, inoffensive type, "Now that

you have made a mess of things, please start over and follow these instructions."

After over fifty years in pastoral ministry, I can say with confidence that most people approach life the same way: "When all else fails, pray." It is part of our fallen, selfish, proud disposition to do things *our* way, and only when the consequences of failure overwhelm us do we seek help.

The disciples noticed that Jesus followed a completely different pattern of prayer. He prayed for different reasons, at different times, with different language, and with a different attitude. After hearing the Lord pray on one occasion, one of His followers asked to learn how to pray like the Son of God.[36]

R. C. Sproul adds:

These men were sensitive enough to notice that Jesus's power was not something that could be learned in three easy lessons. They understood that there was a connecting link between the awesome power that Jesus manifested, and the intense prayer-life to which he gave himself. They made the connection in their minds between the intimacy of Jesus's prayer-life and the power of his ministry. That is a ministry secret, for if you look not only at the ministry of Jesus, but at the ministry of any of the great Christians through the ages, you see this connecting link; those who are powerful in ministry are those who are also earnest in prayer. They know the source of their power.[37]

Application:

Do you have a humble, teachable spirit when learning to pray? Is communicating with God so important that you are willing to sacrifice and train to learn?

Prayer:

Lord, teach me how to pray. I desperately need Your power in my life. Jesus, please help me follow Your example when it comes to communicating with my heavenly Father…

Day 26

START WITH PRAISE

Scripture Reading: Matthew 6:9 (NIV)

> *This, then, is how you should pray: "Our Father in heaven, hallowed be your name."*

Explanation:

Christians have labeled this prayer "The Lord's Prayer," which does not convey the actual intent of His words in Matthew 6. John 17 actually contains the Lord's prayer to His Father and would be a better fit for that title. A more proper title for Matthew 6:9–13 would be "The Disciple's Prayer," because Jesus taught His disciples how to pray in these verses.

Notice that Matthew 6:9 doesn't say, "This, then, is *what* you should pray." Jesus tells His disciples *how* they should pray. Many have taken this Scripture and applied it to quoting the prayer verbatim. Remember, we discussed earlier (Day 19) the difference between saying our prayers and praying them. While it is not necessarily wrong to quote this prayer to God, it was never meant to be recited; instead, it was given as a pattern for prayer. Remember, prayer is a dialogue; quoting a prayer, saying amen, and going about your day cannot be considered a genuine relationship with God.

Jesus's pattern of prayer for His disciples begins with praise. So, our prayers should start with God and not with ourselves. Immature prayers are characterized by someone only giving God a grocery list of requests. Many times, this type of prayer focuses on our wants rather than our needs.

(We will cover this distinction on Day 28.) While God cares about our needs and can meet any of them if He so desires, our time with God should start with worship.

The words *"Our Father in heaven, hallowed be your name"* contain three key aspects of worship.

First, *"Our Father"* shows God's relationship with His children. He is a personal God who desires to be approached. Just as any human father wants his children to talk to and listen to him, our Father God has saved us into a growing relationship where we should know Him better each day.

Second, the two-word phrase *"in heaven"* reminds us that knowing God is unlike any other relationship. God sits on a throne while still desiring to make Himself known. He is supreme, omniscient, omnipotent, and worthy of praise. Therefore, while we are invited into a growing relationship with God at salvation, we never forget that He is to be revered, respected, and adored.

Third, *"hallowed be your name"* reminds us that God is holy. The word used here in the original language means, "to regard as sacred, holy, special, and set apart."[38] God should be praised because of His "otherness." In other words, He is completely set apart as entirely holy and uniquely perfect. We must recognize His purity and power when we approach God in prayer. We are servants entering into the presence of the King of Kings. We are imperfect sinners praying to the Lord God Almighty. We must never approach Him flippantly or irreverently. Every time we enter His presence, we reflect on who God is while remembering all He has done. Prayer should always start with praise.

Application:

How does the beginning of your prayer reflect your reason for praying and your love for God?

Prayer:

Lord, You are worthy to be praised. I exalt Your holy name. Teach me to begin my prayers with praise. Help me never to approach You in a manner that doesn't honor who You are. I do not want to come to You only for my wants and wishes. I need You more than anything…

Day 27

SEEK HIS WILL

Scripture Reading: Matthew 6:10 (NIV)

> *Your kingdom come, your will be done, on earth as it is in heaven.*

Explanation:

Yesterday, we recognized that prayer starts with prayer. After worshipping God, prayer should move to a time of surrender. Remember what you learned from Days 9–11 from Luke 9:23, where Jesus said, *"Whoever wants to be my disciple must deny themselves and take up their cross daily and follow me"* (NIV). Through daily prayer, we deny ourselves of our desires and surrender to His will.

After acknowledging God for who He is, we trust that His plans are much better than ours. For illustration's sake, let's imagine you get to live your life twice. Visualize your first life where you did everything you wanted. You followed your selfish will with every choice you made for your entire life. Now, envision you lived a second full life. However, you surrendered your will this time and followed God's purposes. If you could experience both lives, you would know that your second life would blow your first life away. It would be beyond your imagination how much greater your second life would be because God has way better plans for your life than you would ever choose on your own. We only get one shot at this earthly life, so why waste time outside God's will? Actually, you had a life before Christ. Now that you are a Christian, you have been born again into a new life in Jesus Christ. Now that you are living this new life under His Lordship, you must surrender daily to His will to experience all God has planned.

God did not save you so that you could build your own earthly kingdom. He rescued you from your kingdom of darkness and transferred you to His kingdom of light. (See Colossians 1:13.) He is the only King, and His kingdom is the only thing that matters.

In heaven, all creation worships Jesus and submits to Him as King. Heaven is a perfect place. On Earth, only believers who choose to submit to God's plan find His perfect will. I have often wondered why we are the only part of God's creation that has trouble submitting to God's purpose. God created the sun, moon, and stars. The sun shines, while the moon and stars reflect. God made them, and they fulfill their purpose. God put the fish in the sea and the birds in the air. They all live out God's plan for their existence. Why are people made in God's image (see Genesis 1:27) the only part of God's creation that don't always submit to His Lordship?

That is a question you can resolve personally through an ongoing conversation with God, where you seek His will to be done on Earth exactly as it is in heaven. Praising God daily puts you in the right mindset to continually recognize whose kingdom has the true and rightful King.

Application:

Whose kingdom matters the most to you: yours or Jesus's?

Because you only get one chance at this life, how can your prayer life keep you surrendered to God's will?

Prayer:

Jesus, I praise You for being the only real King. I worship You, for You alone are holy. Today, I submit to Your will and Your ways...

Day 28

ASK GOD TO PROVIDE

Scripture Reading: Matthew 6:11 (NIV)

Give us today our daily bread.

Explanation:

After worshipping Jesus and surrendering to His will, you can be confident that He can and will provide for your daily needs.

When God led His people out of bondage in Egypt, He provided for them at every step of their wilderness wanderings. Exodus 16 enlightens us on God's daily provisions and the need for our constant trust in Him. God gave His people food from heaven with some detailed instructions.

> *Then the LORD said to Moses, "Look, I'm going to rain down food from heaven for you. Each day, the people can go out and pick up as much food as they need for that day. I will test them in this to see whether or not they will follow my instructions. On the sixth day they will gather food, and when they prepare it, there will be twice as much as usual."*
>
> *So Moses and Aaron said to all the people of Israel, "By evening you will realize it was the LORD who brought you out of the land of Egypt." … So the people of Israel did as they were told. Some gathered a lot, some only a little. But when they measured it out, everyone had just enough. Those who gathered a lot had nothing left over, and those who gathered only a little had enough. Each family had*

just what it needed. Then Moses told them, "Do not keep any of it until morning." But some of them didn't listen and kept some of it until morning. But by then it was full of maggots and had a terrible smell. Moses was very angry with them. After this the people gathered the food morning by morning, each family according to its need. And as the sun became hot, the flakes they had not picked up melted and disappeared. On the sixth day, they gathered twice as much as usual—four quarts for each person instead of two. Then all the leaders of the community came and asked Moses for an explanation. He told them, "This is what the Lord *commanded: Tomorrow will be a day of complete rest, a holy Sabbath day set apart for the* Lord*. So bake or boil as much as you want today, and set aside what is left for tomorrow." … The Israelites called the food manna. It was white like coriander seed, and it tasted like honey wafers. Then Moses said, "This is what the* Lord *has commanded: Fill a two-quart container with manna to preserve it for your descendants. Then later generations will be able to see the food I gave you in the wilderness when I set you free from Egypt."*

(Exodus 16:4–6, 17–23, 31–32)

God provided exactly the right amount of manna for the needs of every individual. In addition, He provided for two days in one so they could obey His Word to keep the Sabbath holy. Interestingly, the Bible refers to manna as *"bread from heaven"*:

But he commanded the skies to open; he opened the doors of heaven. He rained down manna for them to eat; he gave them bread from heaven. (Psalm 78:23–24)

In the Old Testament, God's people trusted Him for daily provisions. As we pray daily, we trust that God will give us exactly what we need. This pattern of praying keeps us mindful that as we obey His Word, we have all we need to live in His will.

Application:

Are you too focused on your wants to trust Him for your needs? How can daily trust help your spiritual growth?

Prayer:

Jesus, I adore You as the bread of life. (See John 6:35.) I seek Your will and not my own. I trust that You will provide all my needs as I daily trust in You...

Day 29

FIND FORGIVENESS

Scripture Reading: Matthew 6:12 (NIV)

> *And forgive us our debts, as we also have forgiven our debtors.*

Explanation:

Our regular pattern of prayer should be praise, surrendering to God's will, and trusting God to provide our daily needs. Next, we move to finding forgiveness. We are to forgive others because we have been forgiven. The simple principle is that forgiven people forgive people.

Contemplate the way Jesus tells His disciples to pray by saying aloud: "Father, forgive me of my sins in the same way that I have forgiven others." Do we really want to pray like this? Have we thought about what Matthew 6:12 says? Do we want God to forgive us to the same level that we forgive others? Is this what we truly desire? If we are going to be true to follow the pattern of this prayer, then we better get more serious about forgiving others. We must change our ways or change our prayer!

That is precisely why we don't recite prayers verbatim, where it only means something in our subconscious nature. God gave us the privilege of speaking and listening to Him so that He could transform our lives.

Why would Jesus put forgiveness in this context in the model prayer for all believers? Why not just have us pray, "Father, forgive us because we have sinned." That would be much simpler. However, God always knows best, so He gives this twist on forgiveness. God, the ultimate forgiver, knows that we need to forgive as an act of appreciation for all that we have been forgiven!

Praying that God will forgive us is asking Him to set us free from the debt that sin has placed on our spiritual account. In other words, sin has enslaved us, and finding forgiveness sets us free. This reminds me of a famous quote on forgiveness by Lewis Smedes:

> To forgive is to set a prisoner free and discover that the prisoner was you.[39]

Our Scripture for today and this quote bring together a fascinating truth about forgiveness. Unforgiveness is a sin. If we ask God to forgive us for a sin to set us free while we are still unforgiving towards someone else, then we are putting ourselves back in debt to sin all over again. It's like asking God to set us free while running back into the prison cell as we pray. It doesn't make sense when you think of it that way. Sin is both an attitude and an action. And we can't ask God to forgive us for a wrong action we committed while at the same time harboring sin in our hearts because of an attitude of unforgiveness. It is extremely hypocritical to ask God to do something for us that we aren't willing to do for others.

Application:

Why is it essential to focus daily on God's forgiveness? How should God's forgiveness of your sins change the way you treat others?

Prayer:

Our Father, who art in heaven, I really do want to pray the way You modeled for me in Your Word. But to do that sincerely, I need You to help me forgive others. Help me not to sin by withholding forgiveness from others while I pray for You to forgive me. Thank You for all You are teaching me about prayer…

Day 30

DEPEND ON HIS POWER

Scripture Reading: Matthew 6:13

> *And lead us not into temptation, but deliver us from the evil one.*

Explanation:

Thus far, here is what we have learned from the model prayer found in Matthew 6:9–13:

- Spend time praising God.
- Make sure you surrender to His will.
- Trust Him to provide for your daily needs.
- Accept His forgiveness and find the strength to forgive others.

Of course, prayer involves more than just these areas. Your daily time with God will include interceding for others and yourself. Yet, Jesus taught His disciples that these are the major points of emphasis that must be found in your prayer life if you are to grow in your walk with Him.

Matthew 6:13 gives us insight into one final critical area needed in our prayers to God. We must include time in our communication with God to request and rely on His power over our enemies and temptations.

In his commentary on Matthew, Douglas Sean O'Donnell, explains Jesus's words in Matthew 6:13:

> We need forgiveness of all past sins, but we also need assistance in overcoming any and all future sins. This is why Jesus teaches us next to pray, *"And lead us not into temptation, but deliver us from evil"* (v. 13).
>
> The idea here is *not,* "Lord, please don't bring us to the place of temptation," or "don't allow us to be tempted." We know that God's Spirit brought Jesus into the wilderness to be tempted. (See Matthew 4:1.) So what is being asked here is rather, "Lord, don't let us succumb to temptation," or "don't abandon us to temptation." Here we find a petition for utter dependence on God's providence, protection, and power. It is a prayer of a weak person to a strong God.
>
> All of us must undergo various trials and temptations in order that God might test the authenticity of our faith. We are all tested as if by fire. So, our prayer should be that though tested, we are not consumed.
>
> Temptation is one thing, but evil another. So Jesus teaches that we are to pray not only *"lead us not into temptation,"* but also *"deliver us from the evil one"* (v. 13). The word here for "deliver" can be rendered "snatch." It is a most aggressive word. So here we are asking God, with his divine hand, to snatch us from Satan. "Lord, grab us from the grip of the evil one and his evil ways" is the sense of the prayer.[40]

Our prayer lives should include regularly asking for God's guidance and protection. We need God to shield us from temptations and save us from the tempter.

Application:

How can integrating the subject of Matthew 6:13 in your prayer life keep you vigilant in the fight against temptation?

Prayer:

Jesus, I worship You for You are mighty to save. You alone, Lord, have the power to keep me from temptation. You, and only You, have the power to defeat the enemy. I daily need Your strength, guidance, and protection...

Day 31

STAY FAITHFUL IN PRAYER

Scripture Reading: Colossians 4:2

> *Devote yourselves to prayer with an alert mind and a thankful heart.*

Explanation:

God's Word exhorts us to be faithful and devoted in our prayer lives. The New Testament word for *devote* in Colossians 4:2 is the same word translated as *faithful* in the following verse:

> *Be joyful in hope, patient in affliction, faithful in prayer.*
> (Romans 12:12 NIV)

This word means "to persist and persevere" and "continue steadfast in." This same word is also found in Acts 2:42, which says, "*They* ***devoted*** *themselves to the apostles' teaching and to the fellowship, to the breaking of bread and to prayer*" (NIV).

God never intended for His children to live only in the natural realm. He made us in His own image. That doesn't mean we look like God. We are His image bearers because He created us with a spiritual nature. Not only did God create us with a spirit, but when He saves us, He sends the Holy Spirit to live within us. He wants us to live in the supernatural realm.

God has big plans for His children. For you to live out those plans, you must have His power. To have His power, you must hear His voice. To hear His voice, prayer must be a priority in your life. To live out God's will, you must stay in constant contact with Him.

Isn't it fascinating that God's plan involves a consistent and persistent communication with Him? God loves you so much that He not only wants to save you for eternity, but He wants to strengthen you for today. His power is forever, but He is personal enough for every second along life's journey. God hardwired you for a personal relationship with Him. Your Christian life and mine will never grow higher or deeper than our time in prayer with God.

In Exodus 33:11, we read these words concerning Moses: *"Inside the Tent of Meeting, the LORD would speak to Moses face to face, as one speaks to a friend."* You can learn a valuable lesson from Moses: God wants to talk to you as His friend.

Exodus 33:11 ends with this statement: *"Afterward Moses would return to the camp, but the young man who assisted him, Joshua son of Nun, would remain behind in the Tent of Meeting."* So, learn another prayer lesson from Joshua: Stay faithful in prayer and make sure you don't miss valuable time in His presence!

Application:

As you focus on prayer, how would you assess the current state of your prayer life? Explain your assessment. How can you be more persistent and steadfast in your prayer life? Is your personal life with Jesus, in fact, personal? How do you speak with God as a man speaks with his friend?

Prayer:

Lord, I worship You for being all-powerful yet personal. I submit to Your will and trust You to provide for my needs. Forgive me of my sins as I forgive others who have sinned against me. Give me wisdom to avoid tempting situations and deliver me from the ongoing attacks of the evil one. You are my Savior and best Friend. Keep me faithful in prayer…

Day 32

PRAYER IS A LIFESTYLE

Scripture Reading: Psalm 116:1–2

> *I love the Lord because he hears my voice and my prayer for mercy. Because he bends down to listen, I will pray as long as I have breath!*

Explanation:

God did not give us the privilege of prayer just for life's emergencies. Instead, God granted us access to Him as fuel for daily living. If we are to cultivate a lifestyle of prayer, we must choose to seek the Lord, day by day and moment by moment. Prayer is a way of life for every believer. Martin Luther once said, "To be a Christian without prayer is no more possible than to be alive without breathing."[41]

In Psalm 116, the psalmist equated his love for God with hearing God's voice and calling out to the Lord. Your constant love for the Lord leads to a desire to spend time with Him. Who doesn't want to be in the presence of the one they long for? So, our love for God causes us to want to hear from Him and speak to Him. The more time we spend with God, the deeper we fall in love with Him. The result is a lifestyle of prayer because we incessantly want to be in His presence. Therefore, the longer we walk with Jesus, the deeper our prayer life should grow.

In Psalm 116:2, the psalmist shares an interesting statement: "*Because He bends down to listen.*" God desires to hear our voices. Like a loving father kneeling before his children, God leans down and listens to what you have to say.

One of a million things I love about God is that He wants to listen. Notice the following verses of Scripture:

> *Before they call I will answer; while they are yet speaking I will hear.* (Isaiah 65:24 ESV)
>
> *The LORD is near to all who call on him, to all who call on him in truth.* (Psalm 145:18 ESV)

The Lord is close, and He wants to listen. Why wouldn't you want to cultivate a lifestyle of prayer with Him? Your Creator wants a conversation. Your Savior speaks, and the Lord listens.

The essence of Christianity is a relationship with Jesus Christ. To have life in Jesus Christ, you must have a lifestyle of prayer. If you only pray occasionally, you will have a sporadic relationship with Jesus. You can't expect to pray meaningless words to Him and have a meaningful relationship with Him. Neither can you pray once a week and still have a strong walk with your Lord. It will take a dedicated lifestyle of prayer to have a life devoted to your Lord.

Application:

Is your walk with the Lord characterized by a lifestyle of prayer? If so, in what ways? If not, what needs to change?

What are your thoughts on the following quote, and how does it relate to today's devotion?

> "True prayer is a way of life, not just for use in case of emergency. Make it a habit, and when the need arises, you will be in practice." —Billy Graham[42]

Prayer:

God, I need to seek You wholeheartedly through a lifestyle of prayer. I have nothing to offer in my own strength. I am nothing without You. But in You, all things are possible. Help me to remain in You constantly and to rely on You desperately. Give me a deeper hunger for a relationship with You that keeps me on my knees before You...

Part 5

THE IMPORTANCE OF BIBLE STUDY

Nothing is more important to growing in your relationship with Jesus Christ than daily prayer and study of God's Word. Second Timothy 3:16 begins with these vital words: *"All Scripture is inspired by God."* The word "inspired" is the New Testament word *theópneustos,* a compound Greek word consisting of the words *theós,* "God" and *pnéō,* "breathe out." This word is properly translated as "God-breathed," which is where we get the idea of divine inspiration.[43]

Our Scripture was breathed out by God. Everything in His Word *"is useful to teach us what is true and to make us realize what is wrong in our lives. It corrects us when we are wrong and teaches us to do what is right. God uses it to prepare and equip his people to do every good work"* (2 Timothy 3:16–17).

Since it is God-breathed, Scripture is God's number one way to speak to us. Thus, the depth of your relationship with God will always be directly proportional to the quality time spent in studying the Bible. This means you must do more than just read God's Word. You must study it to show yourself approved. (See 2 Timothy 2:15.) Studying involves meditating, memorizing, understanding the meaning, and applying God's Word to your life.

Over the next six days, we will focus on how vitally important the study of God's Word is to your growth as His disciple.

Day 33

A LIGHT FOR YOUR PATH

Scripture Reading: Psalm 119:105

> *Your word is a lamp to guide my feet and a light for my path.*

Explanation:

As believers, we are called to be the light of the world. (See Matthew 5:14.) To shine God's light, we need to have His light. We live in a world surrounded by spiritual darkness. In this dark world, we need a light to guide us. The psalmist declared that the light we need is God's Word, and it will light our pathway and guide our feet.

Warren Wiersbe explains Psalm 119:105 with these words:

> Two familiar biblical images combine in this verse: life is a path and God's Word is the light that helps us follow the right path. The ancient world did not have lights such as we have today; the people carried little clay dishes containing oil, and the light illuminated the path only one step ahead. We do not see the whole route at one time, for we walk by faith when we follow the Word. Each act of obedience shows us the next step, and eventually we arrive at the appointed destination. We are told that this is "an enlightened age," but we live in a dark world and only God's light can guide us aright. Obedience to the Word keeps us walking in the light.[44]

Notice how this theme of guidance to God's path is connected to God's Word in the following verses of Scripture:

> *The precepts of the Lord are right, giving joy to the heart. The commands of the Lord are radiant, giving light to the eyes.* (Psalm 19:8 NIV)
>
> *I have chosen the way of faithfulness; I have set my heart on your laws.* (Psalm 119:30 NIV)
>
> *I run in the path of your commands, for you have broadened my understanding.* (Psalm 119:32 NIV)
>
> *Direct me in the path of your commands, for there I find delight.* (Psalm 119:35 NIV)
>
> *For this command is a lamp, this teaching is a light, and correction and instruction are the way to life.* (Proverbs 6:23 NIV)

Nothing will light your way and guide your steps better than God's Word. Just as you daily turn the lights on in your house, so you don't walk in darkness, open God's Word often so that you can spiritually see the path that God has for you.

Application:

How important is God's Word to your spiritual growth? How can you commit to studying Scripture on a daily basis? Why is it important that God gives you a passion for hearing His voice?

Prayer:

Lord, today I pray that You will give me a consistent desire to study Your Word. I need Your light to help me follow You. As the psalmist said, *"Show me the right path, O Lord; point out the road for me to follow"* (Psalm 25:4)...

Day 34

ALL SCRIPTURE IS USEFUL

Scripture Reading: 2 Timothy 3:16–17

> *All Scripture is inspired by God and is useful to teach us what is true and to make us realize what is wrong in our lives. It corrects us when we are wrong and teaches us to do what is right. God uses it to prepare and equip his people to do every good work.*

Explanation:

All of God's Word is "*useful.*" This word means "profitable, beneficial, advantageous."[45] It is the same word for "benefit" found in 1 Timothy 4:8:

> *Physical training is good, but training for godliness is much better, promising benefits in this life and in the life to come.*

Studying all of God's Word will give you the greatest advantage in spiritual growth. Learning the Old and New Testaments will be profitable and beneficial for your discipleship. If you want to train for godliness, you must become an avid student of Scripture.

A lawn mower is useful, but if you don't use it, you will have nothing but overgrown grass and weeds in your yard. A toothbrush is helpful, but if you don't brush your teeth, you will get tooth decay. A car is beneficial, but if you don't put gas in it, you will never go anywhere. Likewise, God's Word needs to be read, studied, and meditated on regularly, to prevent spiritual weeds from taking over your life. Scripture needs to be applied so that you will not spiritually decay. If you want to go where God wants you to go spiritually, you must fill your spiritual tank with God's inspired words.

James, the half-brother of Jesus, understood the importance of applying God's Word. He wrote:

> *Do not merely listen to the word, and so deceive yourselves. Do what it says. Anyone who listens to the word but does not do what it says is like someone who looks at his face in a mirror and, after looking at himself, goes away and immediately forgets what he looks like. But whoever looks intently into the perfect law that gives freedom, and continues in it—not forgetting what they have heard, but doing it—they will be blessed in what they do.*
>
> (James 1:22–25 NIV)

If James were writing in today's culture, he would probably say, "Don't let God's Word go in one ear and out the other." This means we can't daydream when it comes to reading God's Word. When the King of all kings speaks to you, your desire should be to pay close attention. When Creator God speaks His will through His Word into your life, you do not easily forget what He says. God doesn't want you to hear His Word. He desires for you to study it intently and live it out continually.

Application:

What is your current approach to God's Word? Is it casual or reverent? Do you listen with great expectation that God wants to teach you more about Himself? How can you become a consistent doer of God's Word?

Prayer:

God, I praise You for revealing Yourself through Your Word. Thank You for the priceless gift of Scripture. Help me to pay close attention when I open Your Word, and give me a passion to apply the Bible daily…

Day 35

FIND YOUR DELIGHT IN HIS WORD

Scripture Reading: Psalm 1:1–3

> *Oh, the joys of those who do not follow the advice of the wicked, or stand around with sinners, or join in with mockers. But they delight in the law of the* Lord*, meditating on it day and night. They are like trees planted along the riverbank, bearing fruit each season. Their leaves never wither, and they prosper in all they do.*

Explanation:

There is a vast difference between feeling like you have to do something and feeling like you get to do it. It is the distinction between duty and desire, or obligation and opportunity. Many Christians claim to love Jesus, but at the same time, admit to not studying God's Word consistently. How can we love God and not long to hear what He has to say?

Anyone who has ever been in love knows the feeling of anticipation when spending time with that special someone. You count down the hours and minutes until you're in their presence again. You go to work but can't get that person off your mind. You are supposed to be working, but you find yourself staring at their picture on your desk. Your heart beats faster each time you see their face. Love responds with eager anticipation and intense expectation.

The same or even stronger experience should be true when it comes to our relationship with Jesus.

First of all, nobody will ever love us to the degree that our Savior loves us. Paul wanted every believer to "*have the power to understand, as all God's people should, how wide, how long, how high, and how deep his* [God's] *love is*" (Ephesians 3:18).

Second, your love for God should be stronger than your love for anyone else. Remember that on Day 16, we examined the greatest commandment, which is to love God with your entire being. (See Matthew 22:37.) Since we know God loves us completely, and we love Him fully, studying the Bible should come from an attitude of extreme desire to spend time with Jesus.

The psalmist used the word "*delight.*" "*But they delight in the law of the Lord, meditating on it day and night*" (Psalm 1:2). "Delight" is a strong word that means "you desire something because it is extremely valuable."[46] The word "*meditating*" implies that you can't get God's Word off your mind. Nothing is more valuable than reflecting on His Word throughout the day.

Notice the contrast between the first two verses in Psalm 1. The first verse discusses the joy one experiences when the world doesn't influence them. The second verse reveals the value of a life that is impacted by the Word of God. Notice how *The Message* translated Psalm 1:2: "*Instead you thrill to God's Word, you chew on Scripture day and night.*"

Psalm 1:3 likens a life built on God's Word to a tree planted by streams of water. If you delight in His Word, your spiritual life will prosper and bear fruit. The key to such a life is cultivating an attitude of delight in your relationship with Jesus. No one should ever have to remind you to spend quality time with the love of your life.

Application:

How important is your love of Jesus to sustaining a vibrant and consistent study of God's Word?

Prayer:

Jesus, nobody will ever love me the way You do! Help me to love You so much that my attitude will always bring anticipation, excitement, and expectation when it comes to spending time with You…

Day 36

FIND YOUR HOPE IN HIS WORD

Scripture Reading: Romans 15:4

> *Such things were written in the Scriptures long ago to teach us. And the Scriptures give us hope and encouragement as we wait patiently for God's promises to be fulfilled.*

Explanation:

We live in a complicated world that is in desperate need of hope. God has given us approximately 7,500 promises in His Word. These vows from God were written in Scripture to "*give us hope and encouragement as we wait patiently for God's promises to be fulfilled*" (Romans 15:4).

Psalm 119 highlights the importance of putting your hope in His Word:

> *May all who fear you find in me a cause for joy, for I have put my hope in your word.* (Psalm 119:74)
>
> *You are my refuge and my shield; your word is my source of hope.* (Psalm 119:114)

In verse 74, the psalmist confesses that he finds hope in God's Word. In verse 114, his hope is so strong in God's Word that he describes God as his hiding place and shield. The Hebrew words for *hope* and *word* are the same in these two verses. *Word* is the Old Testament word *dabar,* and it means, "speech, utterances, or words."[47] Therefore, the psalmist's hope comes from the words God speaks and utters to him. The word for *hope* in these two verses is *yachal.* The primary meaning of *yachal* is "to wait expectantly, to cause to hope."[48] When you know God speaks to you, you can have confidence in your relationship with Him. When you hear His voice, you have confidence that He will guide you to future victories.

Between these two verses, the psalmist offers us this hope-filled Scripture from Day 33 about God's Word: "*Your word is a lamp to guide my feet and a light for my path*" (Psalm 119:105).

When God turns His lamp to shine on your feet, you can take your next step with confidence. When God spotlights your path, you never have to doubt the direction you are headed. Because God knows your future and He lights the way, you can move forward with certainty. His Word gives direction and protection. When you hear Him speak, your hope abounds.

While the Old Testament reveals the hope that comes from God's spoken words, the New Testament extends our hope to His written Word. (See Romans 15:4.) Everything in Scripture was written for the ultimate purpose of bringing hope to our lives. Scripture teaches us about the endurance of others to encourage us to imitate their hope. God has never failed to accomplish His purposes in the past, and He will never fail us in the future. The Bible is filled with examples of people who faced extreme difficulties yet persevered and saw God's promises fulfilled in their lives. Therefore, we have a God who speaks to guide us on our way. In addition, we have a God who inspired Scripture, full of testimonies, so that we can read and be reminded of His power and goodness. We have been given everything we need to hope in His Word.

Application:

How does the following quote encourage your time in God's Word?

> The vigor of our spiritual life will be in exact proportion to the place held by the Bible in our life and thoughts.
>
> —George Muller[49]

Prayer:

God of all hope, thank You for the hope found in Your Word...

Day 37

SEEK DISCERNMENT

Scripture Reading: Proverbs 2:1–6

> *My child, listen to what I say, and treasure my commands. Tune your ears to wisdom, and concentrate on understanding. Cry out for insight, and ask for understanding. Search for them as you would for silver; seek them like hidden treasures. Then you will understand what it means to fear the* Lord*, and you will gain knowledge of God. For the* Lord *grants wisdom! From his mouth come knowledge and understanding.*

Explanation:

King Solomon, inspired by the Holy Spirit, was credited with writing our Scripture for today. Elsewhere, the Bible states that King Solomon was the wisest man who ever lived. (See 1 Kings 3:12; 4:29–34.) When Solomon surrendered to God's will and obeyed His commands, he did amazing things to support and advance God's kingdom. However, his poor decisions ultimately led to his downfall. His life teaches us that wisdom is only useful when applied.

Proverbs 2 challenges us to do these things when it comes to the wisdom of God: listen, treasure, tune your ears, concentrate, cry out for insight, ask for understanding, and search for them like hidden treasures. All of these speak to our desire for God. When we want God's wisdom and guidance more than anything else, we will seek Him with all of our hearts. When we seek Him with all of our hearts, His Word assures us that we will find Him. (See Jeremiah 29:13.)

When we want to hear God more than anyone else, our deep desire will lead to His divine discernment. Proverbs 2:5 states that you *"will understand what it means to fear the LORD, and you will gain knowledge for God."* Scripture did not say, "You might." It says, *"You will."* When your desire for God is strong, His discernment will be sure. Verse 6 reinforces this truth. God grants wisdom. When He speaks to you, out pours His knowledge and understanding.

Many new believers miss this vital step when it comes to studying God's Word. They fail to ask God for discernment. It takes divine discernment to understand all that God wants you to understand from His Word. If you are going to mine the deep treasures of God's Word, you must be desperately dependent on insight from the One who wrote it.

Every time you go to God's Word, you must seek discernment, insight, understanding, and knowledge from God. That is why, before you read a commentary and hear what somebody else said about a Scripture, ask the Author to enlighten you.

God's Word is living and active. (See Hebrews 4:12.) It was never intended to be only studied through second-hand knowledge. God wants to give you first-hand insider knowledge. You should consult commentaries only after you have searched God's Word and sought His wisdom for yourself.

Application:

How is your level of desire for God's discernment when it comes to understanding His Word? How can your desire to know God more personally lead to a deeper understanding?

Prayer:

God, I desperately need Your wisdom as I study Your Word. Help me to always approach Your Word wholeheartedly, entirely dependent on Your guidance. Please impart Your insight and give me discernment...

Day 38

BIBLE STUDY LEADS TO GROWTH

Scripture Reading: 1 Peter 2:1–3

> *So get rid of all evil behavior. Be done with all deceit, hypocrisy, jealousy, and all unkind speech. Like newborn babies, you must crave pure spiritual milk so that you will grow into a full experience of salvation. Cry out for this nourishment, now that you have had a taste of the Lord's kindness.*

Explanation:

From the moment you were saved ("*born again*"—John 3:3), God planned for you to grow spiritually. As a baby physically grows and matures, parents buy larger clothes. Old clothes come off, and newer garments are put on. The same is true spiritually. As you grow up in Christ, you must take off the old fleshly nature and clothe yourself with Jesus Christ. Romans 13:14 commands you to, "*Clothe yourself with the presence of the Lord Jesus Christ. And don't let yourself think about ways to indulge your evil desires.*"

First Peter 2:1 provides a list of the old garments that must be discarded if you are to grow to spiritual maturity. Then, verse 2 connects this baby analogy to what happens to those who are babes in Christ. Regardless of your physical age, if you have recently trusted in Jesus as your Lord and Savior, you are young spiritually. As a baby craves milk and cries when they cannot have it, you should desire the milk of God's Word so you "*will grow into a full experience of salvation.*" Crave is a strong word. Remember how intense your fleshly cravings were before salvation? As a child of God, now your most powerful desire should be for God's Word. You should be crying out for "*this nourishment.*" Notice, verse 2 highlights the fact that salvation is an event followed by a process. God can save you in a moment, but it will take a lifetime for you to fully experience all that salvation entails.

First Peter 2:3 connects back to Psalm 34:8:

> *Taste and see that the* Lord *is good; blessed is the one who takes refuge in him.* (NIV)

The idea is that when we were saved, we experienced a taste of God's goodness. Similar to how taking one bite of your favorite food leaves you craving more, salvation leaves us always hungering for more of Jesus. You cannot taste the goodness of God without it creating an enormous appetite for more of Him.

Bible study is spiritual nourishment for your spiritual nature. You cannot grow as a believer without spending regular time seeking God through His Word. Scripture is the daily sustenance of your soul, as food is to your physical body. Just as you cannot grow physically without the basic requirements of food, Bible study provides the essentials for spiritual growth. Continue to crave God, now that you have tasted His goodness and kindness.

Application:

How is your appetite for God? In what ways do you need to keep craving God so that you can "*grow into the full experience of salvation*" (1 Peter 2:2)?

Prayer:

God, I praise You for Your goodness and kindness. I have tasted and experienced that You are awesome. Help me to crave Your Word more than I desire daily food…

Part 6

SERVING GOD

The two main New Testament words for ministry are *diakoneo* and *douleuo*. The first term means "to serve"[50] and the second translates "to serve as a slave."[51] The biblical concept of ministry has always been closely tied to the idea of service. Therefore, a true disciple of Jesus Christ takes on the posture of a servant.

Another Greek word used for "minister" is *hyperetes*, which literally translates as "the under-rower."[52] This is the word for servant found in the following Scripture:

> *This, then, is how you ought to regard us: as servants of Christ and as those entrusted with the mysteries God has revealed. Now it is required that those who have been given a trust must prove faithful.*
>
> (1 Corinthians 4:1–2 NIV)

This New Testament word for *servant* describes a rower in the bottom of the ship. The rower works hard, but nobody knows that he is down in the lowest section of the ship. Several lessons are gleaned from this word picture. All the servants had to row together in obscurity so that the captain could get to his destination. They worked and labored so that the captain could be honored and recognized. This is an excellent picture of the Christian as a servant of Christ ministering so that God gets the glory He deserves.

God has called us to serve Him! It is a privilege and the real motive for any ministry. Jesus repeatedly modeled servanthood to His disciples. And then He called them to serve the same way He had demonstrated to them.[53] Over the next six days, we will examine Jesus's model of servanthood and His call for His disciples to serve others.

Day 39

SERVING GOD BY FOLLOWING

Scripture Reading: John 12:26

> *Anyone who wants to serve me must follow me, because my servants must be where I am. And the Father will honor anyone who serves me.*

Explanation:

We are never more like Christ than when we are serving Him and others. That's why Scripture makes it clear that for you to serve Jesus, you must follow Him. You can't imitate your Savior if you aren't walking close to Him. You must be where Jesus is so that you can personally witness His servant nature.

This is true in any parent-child, mentor-disciple relationship. A father can show his son how to throw a baseball through a FaceTime video, but it isn't nearly as effective as being there in person.

When I was a young boy, I will never forget my father teaching me how to throw and catch a baseball. I remember him putting the ball in my hand, showing me how to grip it with my fingers, then walking a few steps away and telling me to throw it to him. I vividly remember him holding the glove while it was on my hand, moving it to the proper position, and showing me how to catch a ball. He taught me personally with a hands-on approach, and it made all the difference in how I learned. It also influenced how I taught my boys to do the same.

Likewise, somebody can disciple you by phone or through a video conference, but it is more beneficial if you are there in person to experience and see it modeled. That's precisely why Jesus calls us to serve Him by following Him. The foundational level of serving Jesus Christ begins through faithfully following Him. Some people mistakenly start their attempts to serve Jesus by focusing on what they do for Him. This is the wrong starting point. Jesus wants you to begin your service to Him by staying as close to Him as possible. When you follow Him, you learn about His heart, attitude, life, and actions. The more closely you follow Him, the more precisely you discover how to imitate Him.

When you approach your initial service to God as your commitment to follow Him, Jesus influences and impacts the way you live your life. That approach makes a huge difference in your motives. There is a stark contrast between striving to do things in your own strength for God and loving Him enough to want to spend time with Him. The latter approach leads you to follow Christ's example because He modeled it, not because you are trying to perform for Him from a distance.

John 12:26 concludes with a promise: *"And the Father will honor anyone who serves me."* God honors those who serve God by simply following Him. God saved you so that you could grow to know Him. Don't spend your entire life trying to do things for God and never take the time to follow Him intimately. When you get serving Him in the correct order, you end up living right because you are following His example. However, the result is more than just proper actions; it is a growing relationship.

Application:

How did the Pharisees in Jesus's day miss Him because they were focused more on good words than on a relationship? How does serving God begin with following Him?

Prayer:

Lord Jesus, I know that You desire a personal relationship with Your children. You want to teach me things up close and personal. Help me to never settle for distant discipleship when true service is found in following You…

Day 40

JESUS CAME AS A SERVANT

Scripture Reading: Philippians 2:3–8

> *Don't be selfish; don't try to impress others. Be humble, thinking of others as better than yourselves. Don't look out only for your own interests, but take an interest in others, too. You must have the same attitude that Christ Jesus had. Though he was God, he did not think of equality with God as something to cling to. Instead, he gave up his divine privileges; he took the humble position of a slave and was born as a human being. When he appeared in human form, he humbled himself in obedience to God and died a criminal's death on a cross.*

Explanation:

When Jesus left His throne room in glory, He "*took the humble position of a slave and was born as a human being*" (v. 7). Notice how different translations express how Jesus came:

> *Rather, he made himself nothing by taking the very nature of a servant, being made in human likeness.*
>
> (Philippians 2:7 NIV)

> *When the time came, he set aside the privileges of deity and took on the status of a slave, became human! Having become human, he stayed human. It was an incredibly humbling process. He didn't claim special privileges. Instead, he lived a selfless, obedient life and then died a selfless, obedient death—and the worst kind of death at that—a crucifixion.* (Philippians 2:7–8 MSG)

Jesus set aside His privilege and position, choosing to become a servant, so that you and I could one day choose to be forgiven of our sins and saved for all eternity. Jesus did not simply make this choice once in His coming; He made it repeatedly throughout His life. Having more than one choice makes Him the ultimate example of service. Instead, He continually chose to live as the Son of Man, humbly surrendering to His Father's will. In the Garden, He prayed in anguish as He knew the price He would pay at Calvary. Yet, He chose to serve and submit to God's plan. On the cross, He could have called legions of angels from heaven to rescue Him, yet still He served others rather than saving Himself.

Before Paul describes Jesus's humility and sacrificial service (vv. 6–8), he challenges us to be humble and others-focused, rather than selfish and self-absorbed (vv. 3–4). Interestingly, he follows it with a present active command to *"have the same attitude that Christ Jesus had"* (v. 5). The word translated "attitude" is the New Testament verb *phroneó*. This Greek word originates from a term that means to exercise the mind. The root word is *phroneó*, which means "the midriff or diaphragm; the parts around the heart."[54] So, which one is it, your mind, heart, or attitude? By definition, all three. When your heart is right spiritually and your mind is centered on serving others, your attitude will naturally result in the corresponding behavior that embodies Jesus's servant nature. Since Jesus came as a servant to save us, we must adopt that same mindset to live for Him.

Application:

What does it say about God's character that He came as a servant? What needs to take place in your heart for you to have that same mindset and attitude?

Prayer:

God, I worship You today for humbling Yourself and taking the form of a servant. Please help me to adopt the same attitude towards others…

Day 41

JESUS EXEMPLIFIES SERVICE

Scripture Reading: Mark 10:41–45

> *When the ten other disciples heard what James and John had asked, they were indignant. So Jesus called them together and said, "You know that the rulers in this world lord it over their people, and officials flaunt their authority over those under them. But among you it will be different. Whoever wants to be a leader among you must be your servant, and whoever wants to be first among you must be the slave of everyone else. For even the Son of Man came not to be served but to serve others and to give his life as a ransom for many."*

Explanation:

Mark 10:32–34 records the third time Jesus tells His disciples that He is going to die. This conversation occurs approximately one week before Jesus's death on the cross. What happens next is shocking: Two of Jesus's disciples, James and John, request to sit on either side of Jesus when they reach heaven. Jesus, the Son of God, is about to voluntarily sacrifice His life for the sins of the world, and James and John are worried about their seats in glory.

In response to the selfish question posed by James and John, Jesus makes three significant statements. The first one is in Mark 10:43: "*Whoever wants to be a leader among you must be your servant.*" James and John wanted to become great by sitting next to Jesus in positions of authority for all eternity. Jesus taught them that greatness in His kingdom comes through serving.

Jesus takes His description of greatness to another level when He makes His second statement on servanthood in verse 44: "*Whoever wants to be first among you must be the slave of everyone else.*" God does not measure spiritual success by the number of achievements and awards we possess, but by whether we put others' needs ahead of our own. To be the greatest, God says you must serve others. He used the word slave, which is the Greek word *doulos*. In biblical times, this word described a bond-slave, who had no rights of their own. A *doulos* was "someone who belongs to another." Ironically, this word is used by Paul to describe the honor he felt to willingly give up his rights to serve under God's authority. (See Romans 1:1, Philippians 1:1, and Titus 1:1.)[55]

Jesus concludes His discussion on servanthood with this third declaration in Mark 10:45: "*For even the Son of Man came not to be served but to serve others and to give his life as a ransom for many.*"

In this single sentence, Jesus provided the ultimate purpose statement for His life and ministry. Jesus came to serve and to give His life so that we could be saved. His death on the cross was His chief act of service.

Interestingly, Jesus used the word "*ransom*" to describe His death on the cross. "Ransom" is from the Greek root word *lutron*. This term refers to the price paid to redeem a slave or a firstborn (see Leviticus 25:51–52; Numbers 18:15) or to make restitution and payment for a crime or injury. (See Numbers 35:31–32; Exodus 21:30).[56] When Jesus died on the cross, He paid the price for all of our sins and redeemed us back to Himself. Jesus accomplished all of this for our salvation by becoming a servant. Jesus came to serve and sacrifice Himself for others and has called us to do the same.

Application:

What did you want to be when you were growing up? A policeman, a fireman, an astronaut, a teacher, or a doctor? I have never heard anyone say, "When I grow up, I want to be a servant." How can you make becoming a servant the focus of your Christian life?

Prayer:

God, thank You for being the greatest example of service and for giving Your life as a ransom to pay the price for my sins. Help me to follow Your example and find greatness through serving…

Day 42

BLESSED BY SERVING GOD

Scripture Reading: John 13:12–17

> *After washing their feet, he put on his robe again and sat down and asked, "Do you understand what I was doing?*
>
> *You call me 'Teacher' and 'Lord,' and you are right, because that's what I am. And since I, your Lord and Teacher, have washed your feet, you ought to wash each other's feet. I have given you an example to follow. Do as I have done to you. I tell you the truth, slaves are not greater than their master. Nor is the messenger more important than the one who sends the message. Now that you know these things, God will bless you for doing them."*

Explanation:

John 13 contains one of the most outstanding examples of service found in Scripture. Jesus and His disciples are celebrating the Passover meal just hours before His impending death on the cross. Christ gets up from the meal, grabs a towel and a wash basin, and commences to wash His disciples' feet.

In Jesus's day, the custom of washing feet was a common practice that centered around hospitality and hygiene. People in that period often walked barefoot or in sandals wherever they went. The roads were dirty and dusty. When someone arrived at a house, their feet were filthy. Thus, washing feet was a necessary act to clean their feet and prevent dirt from entering the house. When a guest arrived at your home, it was your customary responsibility to provide a foot-washing service.

Wealthier people would hire servants to do this task, while in poorer homes, the host usually performed this service. So, foot washing represented a service born out of humility.

When Jesus got up to wash His disciples' feet, He was humbling Himself by performing the most menial of services. Jesus washed the feet of Peter, whom He knew would later deny Him. He washed Judas's feet, knowing that he would soon betray Him. Therefore, Jesus served others regardless of whether they loved Him or followed Him. In addition, Christ displayed this humble service at a time when it would have been expected that His disciples would serve Him. Jesus was soon to be beaten beyond recognition, nailed to a cross, and left to suffer for six excruciating hours before His death. No one would have questioned Him if He had taken time out to be served. However, the nature of Jesus is that of a servant.

That nature is passed on to Christ's followers who seek to imitate Him. That's why Jesus said, *"I have given you an example to follow. Do as I have done to you"* (John 13:15). Then He reminded His disciples that a slave is not greater than their master. Since their Master, Jesus, served them by washing their feet, they should have no problem serving others in like manner.

Verse 17 highlights the blessing that results, not from knowing what to do, but from actually engaging in actions of service. The word used for blessed in this verse is *makários,* which means "to become large when God extends His benefits." This word describes a believer being in a fortunate position, having received God's favor.[57] If you want to live beneath the blessings and favor of God, live a life of humble service towards others.

Application:

Imagine Christ washing the feet of His followers. Envision the Master serving His students, the Mentor serving the learners, and the Savior serving the sinners. What does His position disclose about the posture of servanthood?

Prayer:

Jesus, thank You for being a Savior who serves. May Your example of service through washing Your disciples' feet motivate me to serve no matter the situation or the degree of humility required...

Day 43

SERVING ONLY ONE MASTER

Scripture Reading: Matthew 6:24

> *No one can serve two masters. For you will hate one and love the other; you will be devoted to one and despise the other. You cannot serve God and be enslaved to money.*

Explanation:

The Sermon on the Mount comprises 107 verses found in Matthew 5–7. Halfway through this sermon, beginning in Matthew 6:19, Jesus gives a warning about possessions. He teaches that if we value and trust God, then we will store up treasures in heaven for ourselves. Jesus was not against seeking treasure; He just wanted His followers to pursue eternal riches. If we are serving God with the right heart, our focus will not be on what we attain on Earth. Instead, it will be on what we can give in service that will last forever.

Jesus concludes His teaching on possessions with a treasure of truth found in verse 24. Notice that Jesus did not say you might not be able to serve God and money. He said, "*You cannot.*" This can be a hard teaching to accept. Many of us call God the Lord of our lives, yet we devote ourselves to building our lives as we want, buying all the things we want, and doing all the things we want. In Matthew 6:21, Jesus cautions, "*Where your treasure is, there your heart will be also*" (NIV). Our actions reveal our affections. If all we do is spend or save only for ourselves, yet still claim to love God supremely, it reveals that our loyalty is divided. Ultimately, divided loyalty is disloyalty. God wants us to be wholly devoted to Him, and He assures us throughout Scripture that He will provide all the material things we need.

Please note that money is not the root of all evil. The love of money is. Paul addresses this to young Timothy in the following context:

> *Yet true godliness with contentment is itself great wealth. After all, we brought nothing with us when we came into the world, and we can't take anything with us when we leave it. So if we have enough food and clothing, let us be content. But people who long to be rich fall into temptation and are trapped by many foolish and harmful desires that plunge them into ruin and destruction. For the love of money is the root of all kinds of evil. And some people, craving money, have wandered from the true faith and pierced themselves with many sorrows.*
>
> (1 Timothy 6:6–10)

God blesses us with wealth and material goods so that we can honor Him with our giving. If we are not careful, we can be tempted to save God's blessings for ourselves and lose our focus on Him.

You can only have one love in your life. Whoever you love the most will be the one you serve. If your greatest passion is earning worldly wealth, money is your first love. If you love God with all your heart, soul, mind, and strength, then your greatest desire will be to serve Him.

Application:

What do the following quotes teach you about your service and loyalty?

> There can be no part-time loyalty. Jesus wants total devotion. —Bruce Barton[58]

> My aim each day is to adore God more than anything else. —A. W. Tozer[59]

Prayer:

God, I love You and praise You today! I realize I can only serve one Master. May that one always be You…

Day 44

LIVING FOR THE "WELL DONE!"

Scripture Reading: Matthew 25:21, 23

> *The master was full of praise. "Well done, my good and faithful servant. You have been faithful in handling this small amount, so now I will give you many more responsibilities. Let's celebrate together!"...The master said, "Well done, my good and faithful servant. You have been faithful in handling this small amount, so now I will give you many more responsibilities. Let's celebrate together!"*

Explanation:

This parable is a story about talents, stewardship, and the rewards that follow. More specifically, it is a story of buried talents, missed opportunities, and lost rewards. Warren Wiersbe gives the most concise summary of the parable of the talents:

> Note that each servant in this parable was given money (a talent was worth about twenty years' wages) according to his ability. The man with much ability was given five talents; the man with average ability received two talents; the man with minimal ability received one talent.
>
> The talents represent opportunities to use our abilities. If five talents were given to a person with minimal ability, he would be destroyed by the heavy responsibility. But if only one talent were given to a man of great ability, he would be disgraced and degraded. God assigns work and opportunity according to

> ability. We are living in the time between Matthew 25:18 and 19. We have been assigned our ministries according to the abilities and gifts God has given us. It is our privilege to serve the Lord and to steward what He has entrusted to us.
>
> The three servants fell into two categories: faithful and unfaithful. The faithful servants took their talents and put them to work for their Lord. The unfaithful servant hid his talent in the earth. Instead of using his opportunities, he buried them! He did not purposely do evil. But by doing nothing, he was sinning and robbing his Lord of service and increase.
>
> The two men who put their money to work each received the same commendation (Matthew 25:21, 23). It was not the *portion* but the *proportion* that made the difference. They started as servants, but their Lord promoted them to leadership. They were faithful with a few things, so the Lord trusted them with many things. They had worked and toiled, and now they entered into joy. Their faithfulness gave each of them a capacity for greater service and responsibility.
>
> The third servant was unfaithful and therefore was unrewarded.[60]

When Jesus returns, He will hold us accountable for how we served Him with the talents He entrusted to us.

Notice the identical response the two faithful servants received from their master: "*The master was full of praise. 'Well done, my good and faithful servant. You have been faithful in handling this small amount, so now I will give you many more responsibilities. Let's celebrate together!*'" On the day of Jesus's return, the truth will be revealed about how faithfully you served Him. It will be a joyful day when we hear Him say, "*Well done.*"

Application:

If Jesus were to return today, what would you hear Him say?

Prayer:

Jesus, help me to live in such a way that one day I hear You say, "*Well done.*"

Day 45

SERVE HIM BY SERVING OTHERS

Scripture Reading: Matthew 25:31–40

> *But when the Son of Man comes in his glory, and all the angels with him, then he will sit upon his glorious throne. All the nations will be gathered in his presence, and he will separate the people as a shepherd separates the sheep from the goats. He will place the sheep at his right hand and the goats at his left. Then the King will say to those on his right, "Come, you who are blessed by my Father, inherit the Kingdom prepared for you from the creation of the world. For I was hungry, and you fed me. I was thirsty, and you gave me a drink. I was a stranger, and you invited me into your home. I was naked, and you gave me clothing. I was sick, and you cared for me. I was in prison, and you visited me." Then these righteous ones will reply, "Lord, when did we ever see you hungry and feed you? Or thirsty and give you something to drink? Or a stranger and show you hospitality? Or naked and give you clothing? When did we ever see you sick or in prison and visit you?" And the King will say, "I tell you the truth, when you did it to one of the least of these my brothers and sisters, you were doing it to me!"*

Explanation:

We have observed that Jesus is the greatest example of servanthood. If we ask the question, "What Would Jesus Do?", serving others would be the top answer. As we draw closer to Jesus and seek to follow His example, we are challenged to serve others. Rick Warren once said, "The only way you can serve God is by serving other people."[61]

Paul writes about this in his letter to the church in Ephesus:

> *Imitate God, therefore, in everything you do, because you are his dear children. Live a life filled with love, following the example of Christ. He loved us and offered himself as a sacrifice for us, a pleasing aroma to God.*
>
> (Ephesians 5:1–2)

Imitation involves not only copying Jesus's external behavior but also replicating His internal motivation. When we imitate Christ, we serve as He served, and for the same reason. Jesus served others because He deeply loved people. The motivations behind our actions will determine whether we truly imitate Jesus or simply mimic Him.

In Matthew 25, Jesus tells three parables related to His return and the day of judgment. The final one, which is today's Scripture, is called the parable of the sheep and the goats. Jesus uses this story to illustrate the importance of internal motivation. As we read it, we are presented with these questions: When Jesus returns, how will we know if we'll be a sheep or a goat? Will we end up on His right or His left?

To say it bluntly, the sheep are the ones who love others enough to serve them, and the goats are the ones who ignore those with great needs. This truth should inspire us to pray that God will give us a genuine love for others so that we may serve with the right motivation. Furthermore, notice the closing words of the King in verse 40: *"I tell you the truth, when you did it to one of the least of these my brothers and sisters, you were doing it to me!"* In other words, when we serve *"the least of these,"* we are serving Jesus.

Application:

In what ways do you see Jesus in the eyes of the poor and needy? How can you serve Jesus by serving them?

Prayer:

God, I worship You today for being a servant-hearted God. Help me realize that when I serve others, I am actually serving You…

Part 7

WORSHIPPING GOD

There are numerous Hebrew (Old Testament) and Greek (New Testament) words for worship, which illuminate the multifaceted nature of praise. Included is a short list of just Hebrew words for worship, in which I have noted the word as it is used in a passage of Scripture. (All of these were found through www.biblehub.com.)

- Barak—to kneel or bow down. To give reverence to God as an act of adoration.

Come, let us worship and bow down. Let us ***kneel*** *before the* L*ORD* *our maker.* (Psalm 95:6)

- Giyl—to spin around in excitement under the influence of a powerful emotion.

So ***rejoice*** *in the* L*ORD* *and be glad, all you who obey him! Shout for joy, all you whose hearts are pure!*
(Psalm 32:11)

- Hallal—to praise or rave about your adoration of God.

Praise *the* L*ORD*, *all you who fear him! Honor him, all you descendants of Jacob! Show him reverence, all you descendants of Israel.* (Psalm 22:23)

- Yadah—to revere or worship with extended hands.

> *I will* ***thank*** *the* Lord *because he is just. I will sing praise to the name of the* Lord *Most High.* (Psalm 7:17)

This is just a sample of the many reactions of worship found in Scripture. Worship is a response to all God is, says, and does. This response to God comes from our entire created being—heart, mind, emotions, will, and body.

J. I. Packer noted:

> We need to discover all over again that worship is as natural to the Christian, as it was to the godly Israelites who wrote the Psalms, and that the habit of celebrating the greatness and graciousness of God yields an endless flow of thankfulness, joy, and zeal.[62]

We will focus on worship over the next four days. This will provide a brief introduction to a believer's worship, although we cannot cover everything Scripture teaches about worship within this time frame.

Day 46

A CONTINUAL PRIVILEGE

Scripture Reading: Psalm 145:1–2

> *I will exalt you, my God and King, and praise your name forever and ever. I will praise you every day; yes, I will praise you forever.*

Explanation:

Worship is a part of becoming a disciple of Jesus. It is also a byproduct of discipleship. In other words, worshipping God helps us grow in our walk with the Lord. Yet the flip side of the coin is that growing disciples desire to worship Jesus. As you mature as a disciple, you desire to worship the Savior you are following more and more.

When exactly does worship take place in the life of a believer? Do you just turn worship on like a light switch when you come into a church building and have a "worship service"? Of course not. However, we have designated Sunday as the "Worship Hour." We have called the handout with the announcements, "The Worship Guide." We even label the first part of the church service as "Worship Time," followed by time in the Word.

Biblically, we should often remind believers of the following statement: "We don't come to church to worship; we bring our worship to church!" We can't approach worship as if it were something we do only in a church sanctuary on Sunday mornings, just one hour a week. Many people worship God only during a designated time slot labeled as a worship service.

What if every Christian truly worshipped God throughout their workweek, and then all showed up as worshippers at their respective churches on the weekend? What would happen if worship became a daily lifestyle, rather than just a one-time event for every believer? Worship was never to be limited to a church building. And the adoration of God was never meant to be something we just do with our mouths.

Biblical worship is an any-moment, every-day privilege for the believer! First of all, worship can occur at any moment. There is not a moment that goes by that does not contain within it an opportunity to worship.

> *Therefore, let us offer through Jesus a continual sacrifice of praise to God, proclaiming our allegiance to his name. And don't forget to do good and to share with those in need. These are the sacrifices that please God.*
>
> (Hebrews 13:15–16)

True worship is not just any moment, but it is also every day. David declared, *"I will praise you every day; yes, I will praise you forever"* (Psalm 145:2). In the previous verses, did you notice the words *"continually offer"* and *"every day"*? You can make a daily decision to continually offer God praise through the words you say and the way you live. However, worship is a decision you must make.

Worship allows me to connect my personal relationship with God with a passionate response to His greatness. In fact, did you know that you can give God something that He doesn't already have? I know, you think I'm crazy because God already owns everything, right? But there is one thing that God doesn't have unless you give it to Him. And that is the praise from your lips and the worship of your life. No one can give God your personal worship except you. Don't pass up opportunities to bless His name and to worship Him in spirit and in truth. Make a daily decision to devote yourself to the worship of almighty God.[63]

Application:

In what specific ways can you continually offer praise to God?

Prayer:

God, my love for You should be strong enough to lead me to worship You frequently…

Day 47

TRUE WORSHIP

Scripture Reading: John 4:23–24

> *But the time is coming—indeed it's here now—when true worshipers will worship the Father in spirit and in truth. The Father is looking for those who will worship him that way. For God is Spirit, so those who worship him must worship in spirit and in truth.*

Explanation:

In Jesus's conversation with a Samaritan woman, Jesus made it clear that there is both true worship and false worship. Jesus is seeking "*true worshipers.*" The Pharisees in Jesus's day thought they were practicing excellent worship, but in Matthew 15:8–9, Jesus quoted Isaiah to indicate how He saw their "worship":

> *These people honor me with their lips, but their hearts are far from me. Their worship is a farce, for they teach man-made ideas as commands from God.*

Jesus cautioned the religious crowd about the dangers of false worship. If we are not careful, we will miss true worship because our hearts are far from God.

Jesus is looking for true worshippers right now. He describes them with these words: "*True worshipers will worship the Father in spirit and in truth.*"

True worshippers must worship in spirit. True worship gets past the physical and engages the spiritual. If we only praise God in the physical realm of what we see and feel, then worship will not be transformational. That is why singing songs and listening to a sermon don't necessarily constitute worship. Putting our bodies through the physical motions of sitting in a pew and moving our lips to sing a song doesn't amount to worship. We who are born of the Spirit offer true worship only when we engage with God's Spirit that dwells in us.

Warren Wiersbe adds these helpful comments:

> "God is Spirit." It is impossible to offer acceptable worship apart from the Spirit of God. If my inner being isn't yielded to the power of the Spirit, then my worship will only be a demonstration of fleshly zeal fueled by human emotion.[64]

Jesus also said that true worshippers must worship in truth. "*Worshiping in truth*" means having a clear and true understanding of who God is, and who I am in relation to Him, all of which is revealed by reading and understanding the Word of God. Wiersbe writes:

> Both the Spirit and the Word are called "truth" in Scripture. (See 1 John 5:6; John 17:17.) The Spirit of truth wrote the Word of truth that reveals Christ the truth. (See John 14:6.) If I try to worship Jesus Christ apart from the Spirit and the Word, I am destined to fail; but many people attempt it, and some think they succeed. If I am not obeying the truth of the Word of God, what I call "worship" will be nothing but superstition, no matter how good it feels or how many people applaud it.[65]

Application:

In what ways do I currently worship God in spirit and truth? Are there any changes that need to be made in how I worship Him? If so, what are they?

Prayer:

God, I praise You because You are the way, the truth, and the life. (See John 14:6.) Help me to always worship You in spirit and truth...

Day 48

WHATEVER YOU DO

Scripture Reading: 1 Corinthians 10:31

> *So whether you eat or drink, or whatever you do, do it all for the glory of God.*

Explanation:

I long to be a "whatever you do" believer. I found three times in Scripture where Paul makes that statement. Besides the 1 Corinthians 10:31 verse above, here are the other two:

> *And whatever you do or say, do it as a representative of the Lord Jesus, giving thanks through him to God the Father.* (Colossians 3:17)
>
> *Work willingly at whatever you do, as though you were working for the Lord rather than for people.* (Colossians 3:23)

Since worship is a response to who God is and all that He does, we always have a reason to worship Him. We worship God with our lips and our lives, irrespective of life's circumstances. While we will face uncertainties throughout our earthly lives, God never changes. (See Hebrews 13:8.) Regardless of our occupation, we are all called to glorify God. "*Whatever you do,*" make sure you worship, honor, and bring glory to God.

First Corinthians 10:31 must be taken in context. This verse is part of a larger discussion by the apostle Paul addressing the behavior of Christians, particularly in relation to eating food offered to idols. Paul emphasizes that believers must make choices that reflect their faith in Christ. While Christians are free to participate in certain activities, they should always consider the impact their actions have on others. Our actions have profound impacts on the faith of weaker Christians. Therefore, even the mundane things, such as eating and drinking, should be done with a goal of glorifying God.

Worship encompasses so much more than most Christians realize. God never meant worship to be an occasional experience for Christians. If we are to approach every situation as an opportunity to glorify God, then we have limitless occasions to worship Him. This opens up a whole new outlook on life. I can glorify God when I'm brushing my teeth, driving to work, sitting in school, at the office, or in my living room. When I've had a terrible day, I can react in a way that honors God. If I had the best day ever, I could glorify God with an attitude of gratitude.

This raises a profound truth about worshipping God. There is never a time in your life when you can't worship Him. Often, our worship of God is closely tied to our emotions. This is dangerous because when your feelings are hurt, you may miss the opportunity to glorify God. Worship is not based on feelings, but on the facts about who God is. He is who He is, no matter what type of day you have experienced. You can always worship God because He is always worthy of praise. "*Whatever you do,*" make sure you give God glory!

Application:

Why is worship a choice regardless of circumstances? How are you doing at worshipping God from a "*whatever you do*" perspective?

Prayer:

God, I worship You as the never-changing God. In this ever-changing world, I am grateful that I can always trust You. Help me to become a "*whatever you do*" Christian so that I don't miss opportunities to bring glory to Your name...

Day 49

A LIVING SACRIFICE

Scripture Reading: Romans 12:1–2

> *And so, dear brothers and sisters, I plead with you to give your bodies to God because of all he has done for you. Let them be a living and holy sacrifice—the kind he will find acceptable. This is truly the way to worship him. Don't copy the behavior and customs of this world, but let God transform you into a new person by changing the way you think. Then you will learn to know God's will for you, which is good and pleasing and perfect.*

Explanation:

Today's Scripture denotes worship that God finds acceptable. It is worship where we offer our bodies as a living and holy sacrifice. We often overlook the concept of sacrifice when discussing worship. Many people won't sacrifice their day off from work to worship the Lord. Sometimes, people who call themselves Christians aren't willing to sacrifice temporary things to worship the eternal God. Some people only worship God when it is easy and convenient. Yet, Scripture declares that our lives are to be a living sacrifice of worship to God.

Let's be honest. It is easier to attend church and worship God with our lips, yet never praise Him with our lives. However, if we love God more than anything else in life, our lives are the first things we should surrender to Him. A. W. Tozer once said, "No man gives anything acceptable to God until he has first given himself in love and sacrifice."[66]

Leon Morris, in *The Pillar New Testament Commentary*, describes Paul's imagery in Romans 12:1 as follows:

> The appeal is that the readers *offer* their *bodies* as *sacrifices*, a suggestion whose force would be more obvious to Paul's first readers than to most modern students. First-century people were familiar with the offering of sacrifices whereas we are not. They had stood by their altar and watched as an animal was identified as their own, as it was slain in the ritual manner, its blood manipulated, and the whole or part of the victim burned on the altar and ascended in the flames to the deity they worshipped. To suggest that they should be sacrifices was a striking piece of imagery.[67]

We are to offer our bodies as living sacrifices, not as a one-time act of worship, but as the reasonable and proper way to worship God. The NIV translates the last phrase of verse 1 as, "*this is your true and proper worship.*" How you and I live our lives is our spiritual worship.

Romans 12:2 connects worship and offering our bodies as living sacrifices to God, transforming us by changing the way we think. Part of a sacrifice of praise involves a proper mindset. When our thinking is worldly, we cannot worship God appropriately. However, as God renews our minds, we can surrender our bodies and the accompanying actions as acts of worship to God.

Application:

How can you offer your body as a living and holy sacrifice to God? How does the following quote on worship from Eugene Peterson challenge you today?

> "Worship does not satisfy our hunger for God; it whets our appetite."[68]

Prayer:

Lord, You are perfect in holiness and worthy of all praise! Please renew my mind daily and transform my life into one that is a sacrifice of praise to You...

Part 8

FINDING COMMUNITY

When God saved you, you were born again into a new family. In this family, God is your Father. Recorded for us in Scripture, Jesus referred to God as Father over 165 times. The concept of a "family of faith" is a significant theme in Scripture, particularly in Paul's letters. Notice the family theme in the following verses:

> *So now you Gentiles are no longer strangers and foreigners. You are citizens along with all of God's holy people. You are members of God's family.* (Ephesians 2:19)
>
> *You received God's Spirit when he adopted you as his own children. Now we call him, "Abba, Father." For his Spirit joins with our spirit to affirm that we are God's children.* (Romans 8:15–16)

Additionally, the words "church" and "assembly" appear 118 times in Scripture, referring to both the universal church and local congregations. God instituted His church because He never intended for you to live your Christian life in isolation.

It is sad when you hear many people today say, "I can be a Christian and not attend a church." While this is technically true, I would dare say that you cannot be a growing Christian apart from His family. I have even heard people say, "I love Jesus, but I don't have anything to do with His church." To that statement, I would say, "The church is the bride of Christ" (see 2 Corinthians 11:2; Revelation 21:2) and "Jesus died for the church." (See Ephesians 5:25.) How would you feel if someone said, "I love you, but I can't stand your spouse"? And, how can we say we love Jesus but harbor ill feelings for the church that He so loves?

God created us for relationships. As you will see over the next four days, we need the community found in the local church, where we serve and belong to a faith family.

Day 50

MODEL OF THE EARLY CHURCH

Scripture Reading: Acts 2:42–47 (NIV)

> *They devoted themselves to the apostles' teaching and to fellowship, to the breaking of bread and to prayer. Everyone was filled with awe at the many wonders and signs performed by the apostles. All the believers were together and had everything in common. They sold property and possessions to give to anyone who had need. Every day they continued to meet together in the temple courts. They broke bread in their homes and ate together with glad and sincere hearts, praising God and enjoying the favor of all the people. And the Lord added to their number daily those who were being saved.*

Explanation:

Acts 2 ends with a description of how the church lived out their faith! These verses reveal God's plan for His church and detail how the early church made disciples! There are five focuses of the early church disclosed in these verses: worship, evangelism, discipleship, fellowship, and ministry. I have outlined the verses that address each of these five areas:

- Worship
  - » *Everyone was filled with awe at the many wonders and signs performed by the apostles.* (v. 43)
  - » *...praising God...* (v. 47)

- Evangelism
    - » *And the Lord added to their number daily those who were being saved.* (v. 47)
- Discipleship
    - » *...devoted themselves to the apostle's teaching...and to prayer.* (v. 42)
- Fellowship
    - » *...and to fellowship, to the breaking of bread...* (v. 42)
    - » *All the believers were together and had everything in common.* (v. 44)
    - » *Every day they continued to meet together in the temple courts. They broke bread in their homes and ate together with glad and sincere hearts.* (v. 46)
- Ministry
    - » *They sold their property and possessions to give to anyone who had a need.* (v. 45)

This was the model for discipleship for the early church. And it worked! Three thousand people got saved to start the process. As the early church focused on relationships for discipleship, the Lord continued to add "*to their number daily those who were being saved.*"[69]

The early church shared life by belonging to a community of believers. Notice how much of Acts 2:42–47 falls under the category of fellowship. The word for fellowship in these verses is *koinonia,* which means "that which is shared in common as the basis of partnership."[70] Every believer needs this community to grow as a disciple of Jesus Christ.

Application:

How does the current culture's approach to the church differ from that of the early church?

Prayer:

Lord, thank You for saving me into a family of faith, where I have a heavenly Father and brothers and sisters in Christ. Please help me find a place to belong in a community of growing believers...

Day 51

WE ARE BETTER TOGETHER

Scripture Reading: Ecclesiastes 4:9–12

> *Two people are better off than one, for they can help each other succeed. If one person falls, the other can reach out and help. But someone who falls alone is in real trouble.*
>
> *Likewise, two people lying close together can keep each other warm. But how can one be warm alone? A person standing alone can be attacked and defeated, but two can stand back-to-back and conquer. Three are even better, for a triple-braided cord is not easily broken.*

Explanation:

If you have a bonfire going and take a pitchfork to carefully remove a branch from the flames, it won't take long before that branch is no longer burning. Likewise, if Satan can isolate you from other believers, it is much easier for your fire to go out for the Lord. Don't ever forget that Satan desires to steal, kill, and destroy. (See John 10:10.) His number one strategy is to divide and conquer.

Every soldier knows strength comes in numbers. Try playing basketball by yourself against five members united together as a team. You have no chance of winning. Take a single cord and test it against three cords twisted together into one. The triple-braided cord is three times as strong and "*not easily broken*" (Ecclesiastes 4:12).

God declares in His Word that "*two people are better off than one*" (Ecclesiastes 4:9). A team helps individuals succeed in fulfilling God's purpose for their lives. Whereas the NLT has *"succeed,"* the NIV translates verse 9 as *"they have a good return for their labor."* The Message says, *"It's better to have a partner than go it alone. Share the work, share the wealth."*

Take any task and do it alone, then compare how much faster you can accomplish it with help from others. I live on a private twelve-acre lake owned by my in-laws. I often must take my string trimmer and cut down the weeds around the entire circumference of the lake. It is not my favorite task, but it has to be done. Imagine my joy when my three sons each grab a weed eater and help me. We accomplish the same task in a fourth of the time it takes me to do it by myself. It is so much easier, as I am more motivated by seeing their progress around me.

Likewise, Christians are better together. Together, we find encouragement and strength to be all God has called us to be. Together, we learn from others around us. Teamwork develops character and challenges us to grow in our spiritual walk.

I love the word picture in verse 11: *"If one person falls, the other can reach out and help. But someone who falls alone is in real trouble."* Living the Christian life is not easy, but the benefits far outweigh the sacrifices. In our spiritual journey, sometimes we fall. When we start to wander and get distracted in our walk with the Lord, we need believers who will reach out and pick us up.

Peter would have been in real trouble if he tried to walk on water with no one close by. Judas's downfall began the moment he associated with the wrong crowd. Ensure that you remain committed to a community of believers who share your desire to grow in the faith. Remind yourself every time you are tempted to go it alone that you are better together with brothers and sisters in Christ.

Application:

How does Satan tempt you towards isolation? What does today's Scripture say about the advantage of Christian community?

Prayer:

Lord, I praise You for Your plan for believers to be in a family of faith, a community of believers that provides strength and encouragement for one another…

Day 52

WE NEED EACH OTHER

Scripture Reading: 1 Corinthians 12:18–21, 27

> *But our bodies have many parts, and God has put each part just where he wants it. How strange a body would be if it had only one part! Yes, there are many parts, but only one body. The eye can never say to the hand, "I don't need you." The head can't say to the feet, "I don't need you."... All of you together are Christ's body, and each of you is a part of it.*

Explanation:

In 1 Corinthians 12, Paul likens the church (the body of Christ) to our physical bodies. In our natural bodies, God has placed each part exactly where it needs to be. Imagine what life would be like if your eyes were located where your ears are. How difficult would it be for you to walk on your hands and pick up things with your feet? How crazy would it be if our heads and bottoms were swapped? (I don't even want that picture in my mind!) Creator God perfectly fashioned us with all the parts in our body, particularly placed for a specific purpose.

In the same way, God placed each of us into His church for a special purpose. Each one of us is a member of the greater body of believers. Some are hands in the church that serve others. Others are feet in His body, going and sharing the good news of Jesus Christ. Christ is the head of His body, and we are all necessary parts united with the same goal—to glorify God. We all need each other.

I believe that God also precisely places us in our local church. God sends teachers to each church that train us in His Word. God directs prayer warriors to each church to lift believers to God's throne of grace. The Lord places those gifted with service and ministry and apportions them where needed. If we are all where we are supposed to be and serving in our areas of giftedness, then the local church will be all that God has called us to be.

That is why assembling regularly as His church carries both privileges and responsibilities. If a leg in the body is not where it is supposed to be, then we are only standing on one leg as His church. It is much more challenging to move forward as His followers if we are hopping instead of running. If half of the toes don't show up on Sunday, then the church's ministry is out of balance.

Paul specifically says that no part of God's body can ever say, *"I don't need you,"* because we are all desperately dependent upon one another. This truth is supported by approximately fifty-nine unique *"one another"* New Testament passages that provide specific instructions for believers on how to interact. These verses emphasize the importance of mutual service, love, and encouragement within the Christian community. The author of Hebrews emphasizes the importance of gathering with fellow believers:

> *And let us not neglect our meeting together, as some people do, but encourage one another, especially now that the day of his return is drawing near.* (Hebrews 10:25)

When Jesus returns for His Bride, the church, may we all be found fulfilling His calling as a member of His body.

Application:

How are you doing as a part of Christ's body? What is your role, and where is He leading you to serve?

Prayer:

Jesus, thank You for Your plan and purpose given to Your church. Help me understand how You specifically gifted me and exactly where You desire for me to belong in community with other believers...

Day 53

MOTIVATING LOVE IN OTHERS

Scripture Reading: Hebrews 10:24

> *Let us think of ways to motivate one another to acts of love and good works.*

Explanation:

When you belong to a community of believers, you have the opportunity to influence others while also receiving motivation for Christ-like living. The writer of Hebrews encourages believers to "*think of ways*" to motivate one another toward love and good works. The New Testament verb used here is *katanoeó* and means "to think from up to down towards a conclusion." This is a strong word used fourteen times in Scripture, meaning "concentrating your thinking by considering closely and understanding clearly."[71]

Notice how this same verb is used in Acts 7:30–32:

> *Forty years later, in the desert near Mount Sinai, an angel appeared to Moses in the flame of a burning bush. When Moses saw it, he was amazed at the sight. As he went* ***to take a closer look****, the voice of the* Lord *called out to him, "I am the God of your ancestors—the God of Abraham, Isaac, and Jacob." Moses shook with terror and did not dare to look.*

If we want to see God work and experience holy moments with Him, as Moses did, we will need to focus our minds and fix our thoughts on discovering ways to motivate one another to walk faithfully with the Lord.

The Greek word for "motivate" is *paroxusmos,* which means "to provoke, stir up, and incite. It is an interesting word that can also mean "to provoke someone so severely that they must respond."[72] It is found only one other time in the New Testament, in the following Scripture, where Paul and Mark disagreed so intensely that they went their separate ways.

> *Their* ***disagreement was so sharp*** *that they separated. Barnabas took John Mark with him and sailed for Cyprus.* (Acts 15:39)

Thus, the positive aspect of this verb is applied in Hebrews 10:24; yet, as *"think of ways,"* it also implies an intense action. When you put these two words together, Scripture is showing the extreme effort we should make to inspire other believers to two crucial areas: showing love and doing good.

Every athlete knows how exciting and contagious it is to have momentum on your side. Some call it the "Big Mo," which can entirely change the outcome of any game. When momentum is not on your side, nothing seems to go right, and everyone on your team feels discouraged. However, for example, in a basketball game, when momentum is on your side, everyone's shots are going in, and players are feeding off the enthusiasm and success of each other. As a former athlete, I know sports are most fulfilling during these moments.

In a much more significant environment, the same principle applies as Christians encourage and inspire one another to live their best life for Jesus. This level of community leads to the most fulfilling life because it is lived with and for Jesus Christ.

Application:

How can you think of ways to motivate one another to acts of love and good works?

Prayer:

Jesus, I am thrilled that You saved me and placed me in a family of believers where I can both encourage and be encouraged in my daily walk with You…

Part 9

FINAL WORDS TO HIS FOLLOWERS

A person who is dying doesn't waste words. On the contrary, some of the greatest statements ever made were made by people as they took their final breaths. Here are a few of those powerful declarations:

> *"Father, into your hands I commit my spirit."* (Luke 23:46 NIV) —Jesus
>
> *"Look, ... I see heaven open and the Son of Man standing at the right hand of God"* (Acts 7:56 NIV) —Stephen
>
> "The best of all is, God is with us!"[73] —John Wesley
>
> "This is no dream. It is beautiful. If this is death, it is sweet. God is calling me, and I must go. Don't call me back."[74] —D. L. Moody

While these are profound words, no one is greater than Jesus Christ. Therefore, His final words to His followers are among the greatest statements ever made. And, His final statements, which we are about to study, were given after He rose from the grave on the third day! You could say that these are His double final words, because He was resurrected to pronounce them. In addition, we have a living Lord who knows full well whether or not we are obeying His commands.

Over the final week of our journey together, we will study Jesus's final commands that challenge every follower of Christ. We will spend six days carefully examining Matthew 28:16–20, and our final day will focus on Acts 1:8.

Day 54

MOUNTAINTOP MEMORIES

Scripture Reading: Matthew 28:16 (NIV)

> *Then the eleven disciples went to Galilee, to the mountain where Jesus had told them to go.*

Explanation:

Sometimes, people refer to their greatest moments with the Lord as "mountaintop experiences." Several mountaintop moments are recorded in Scripture: Moses was on top of a mountain when God gave him the Ten Commandments (see Exodus 19:3); Elijah was on the top of Mount Carmel when God sent down fire from heaven (see 1 Kings 18:20); and Jesus often met His disciples at the Mount of Olives (see Luke 22:39). In fact, it was there that Jesus gave His final words before ascending to the Father. (See Acts 1:8.) Jesus's greatest sermon is known as the Sermon on the Mount. (See Matthew 5.) Jesus was transfigured before His disciples on what is now known as the Mount of Transfiguration. (See Matthew 17:1–2.) The temple at Jerusalem will one day be located on heavenly Mount Zion. (See Hebrews 12:22–23.)

And here in Matthew 28:16, Jesus gives one of His final words to His followers on a mountain. We know His charge as the Great Commission. (See Matthew 28:18–20.) What better place to shout His final instructions than from the top of a mountain? This mountaintop moment would be forever marked in the minds of Jesus's first disciples. It should be indelibly engraved on the hearts and minds of everyone who calls themselves Christians. In addition, what Jesus said on this mountain should cause us to shout His good news and echo it off every mountaintop.

I would suggest that your mountaintop experiences with Jesus hinge on your obedience to the commands that He gave from that mountain. How could followers of Christ expect God to work in their lives if they fail to obey His final words?

Imagine a patriarch writing his last will and testament for his children. After his death, his children gather for the reading of the will. Though they are sad because they lost their father, they are also anxious about what their father left them, along with a passion to hear his last words. The will is read, and the inheritance given, but with a decree that they had to obey the father's final orders to receive their father's full reward. Since it was an incredible inheritance, you would expect every child to carry out their father's wishes.

Well, every born-again believer is a joint heir with Jesus. There is no greater inheritance than that, except to also hear God say, *"Well done, my good and faithful servant"* (Matthew 25:21, 23). Not to mention, Jesus ascended to the top of a mountain to give His final marching orders to His church. Every child of God would be crazy and irresponsible not to obey those commands. So from this mountaintop, let's carefully observe Jesus's final commands so that we can obey them fully. And, by doing so, we can have some of the greatest mountaintop moments and memories with our Savior and Lord.

Application:

How important is it that Jesus gave His Great Commission from atop a mountain? What does this signify and symbolize in your walk with the Lord?

Prayer:

God, help me to live out Your final commands to all Your disciples. Thank You for making them clear and reminding me daily to obey…

Day 55

WORKING THROUGH DOUBTS

Scripture Reading: Matthew 28:17 (NIV)

> *When they saw him, they worshiped him; but some doubted.*

Explanation:

The first disciples of Jesus Christ are the distinguished guests of this mountain meeting. The command to make disciples was given to the first group that Jesus discipled. Jesus had modeled discipleship to them. Now they were called by Jesus to go and make disciples of others. That commission has been handed down to every follower of Jesus Christ.

Notice how verse 17 begins. "*When they saw him, they worshiped him.*" "*They,*" meaning all eleven disciples (see Matthew 28:16), worshipped Him. When they saw the risen Savior, worship was their automatic response. Worship is a response to God's revelation of Himself. When our worship is real, our witness will be right! You can't help but tell others about Him when you have spent time personally praising the Lord.

Matthew 28:17 ends with a startling statement, "*but some doubted.*" This is at least the fourth resurrection appearance of Jesus to His disciples. Yet some still doubted. Did they still doubt that He was risen and alive? Or did they doubt their ability to carry on as His disciples? If indeed it was the latter, Jesus will give them some incredible confidence and enough encouragement with how He both begins and ends His Great Commission.[75]

Interestingly, Scripture says "*they*" worshipped Him, but "*some*" doubted. It is as if God's Word is hinting that they all worshipped Him, while at the same time, some of those worshippers were still working through their doubts. Aren't you glad to know that you can bring your worship to Jesus no matter what struggles you face? If your faith is weak, worship Him. When your life seems to be falling apart, praise His name. When fears overwhelm you, get alone in His presence and adore Him. Sometimes, you must worship God through your uncertainties to gain greater confidence in trusting Him. So, worship through your doubts.

I love that Jesus didn't divide the crowd into two groups: those who faithfully believed and those who fearfully doubted, and then only gave His commission to those who had no doubts. Observe that Christ gave the same commission to all His disciples. Our Lord doesn't just commission faithful believers and prayer warriors; He calls every believer, regardless of their stage in the faith journey, to obey His commands. Therefore, work through your doubts by following His Word, even when you are experiencing spiritual growing pains.

Application:

In what ways can you worship God for who He is, bring your doubts honestly before Him, and thank Him for all He has done?

Prayer:

God, I honestly struggle with doubts, so increase my faith in You. I realize that I can't wait until I reach spiritual maturity to worship You. Instead, worshipping You with sincerity and honesty helps me grow in my faith. I love You; help me to love You more. I believe; help my areas of doubt...

Day 56

THE POWER BEHIND YOUR CALL

Scripture Reading: Matthew 28:18 (NIV)

> *Then Jesus came to them and said, "All authority in heaven and on earth has been given to me."*

Explanation:

Matthew 28:18 records Jesus's first words of His commission. Christ said, *"All authority in heaven and on earth has been given to me."* Two main Greek words in the New Testament mean "power" or "authority." One of those words is *dunamis.*[76] This is where we get our English word dynamite. This word means "power, might, and force." However, that is not the word found in Matthew 28:18. The word for authority in this text is fascinating. It is the Greek word *exousia.* This is a term that means "the power of influence. The power of him whose will and commands must be submitted to by others and obeyed."[77] It comes from two Greek words: *ek,* meaning "out from," and a form of the verb *eime,* which is the action word "to be." *Eime* is the main verb for the I AM statements of Jesus found in John's Gospel. If you take these two words together, *exousia* is defined as "Out of who I am." God has all authority in heaven and on Earth because of who He is. Out of all that Jesus is, He gives the divine demand to His disciples. As you would expect, Jesus gives an incredible introduction to His Great Commission.[78]

God gives His power to believers to fulfill His calling. You have not been given a task that you are incapable of accomplishing. God's power and might have endowed you with the resurrection power of Jesus. All of God's authority has been gifted to you. You should never say "I can't" when the power behind your calling is the authority of Jesus.

Isn't it comforting to see that three-letter word *"all"*? I mean, let's be honest, some of God's power and authority is more powerful than all our strength combined. Yet, Jesus didn't give His followers some of His might; He gave them all of it!

Paul said in Ephesians 4:4–6 (NIV):

> *There is one body and one Spirit, just as you were called to one hope when you were called; one Lord, one faith, one baptism; one God and Father of all, who is over all and through all and in all.*

The God who is over it all works all of His power through every believer who is submitted to His Lordship. God always empowers and equips His children to obey His commands. Jesus will never call you to do something that He won't enable you to accomplish. The key is not striving in your own strength but yielding yourself and allowing God to work through you to accomplish His purpose.

Application:

Out of who He is, the Great I AM empowers you to fulfill His calling. How does it encourage you that Jesus endows all of His authority from heaven and on Earth to you to obey the Great Commission? How does this truth rid you of any excuses for not obeying His commands?

Prayer:

God, all Your authority is more than enough power for me to live out Your will for this life You have blessed me with. I submit to Your will and yield to Your power. Work in me and through me for Your honor and glory...

Day 57

"MAKE DISCIPLES"

Scripture Reading: Matthew 28:19 (NIV)

> *Therefore go and make disciples of all nations, baptizing them in the name of the Father and of the Son and of the Holy Spirit.*

Explanation:

There are five commands found here in this section of Scripture. Only one of them is the main verb and the divine demand. We will discuss the first three today, the fourth tomorrow, and the last one on Day 59. For better understanding and insight, we will study them in order.

The first command is "Go." In the original language of Greek, the part of speech, tense, and voice of a word reveal a great deal about God's intended meaning. For instance, "go" is plural, meaning all disciples are to go. It is a passive participle, so this command is correctly translated as "having gone." God already expects His followers to be in motion to make disciples. This can also mean that everywhere you go creates an opportunity for you to make disciples.

The second of these four verbs is the main imperative of the Great Commission: "*make disciples.*" The word "make" is not in the original language. Translators add it to help the sentence flow better. It is simply the verb form of "disciple." Jesus tells His first disciples to "Go and disciple!"

A study of this verb, translated as "*make disciples,*" offers us the following insights and applications. It is in the active voice, which means do it right now! The verb is in the imperative form, meaning it is not optional for the believer. It is a command. Like "go," it is plural, so it is for all Christ-followers. And the tense implies it was a once-and-for-all command that God still expects us to obey today and in the future!

This verb is where the word "mathematics" is derived and denotes "the mental effort needed to think something through." To disciple someone means to help someone progressively learn the Word of God and practically live it out in everyday life. It has been defined as "to train (develop) in the truths of Scripture and the lifestyle required, i.e. helping a believer learn to be a disciple of Christ in belief and practice."[79] Therefore, becoming a disciple occurs through a belief that leads to a corresponding behavior.

The third verb is "*baptizing.*" Here, it is found in the present active tense. When you put all this together, here is what Jesus commands: "Having gone, make disciples by baptizing people in the name of the Father, and of the Son, and of the Holy Spirit."

Baptizing is the beginning part of the process of discipleship, not the ending.[80] Nowhere in Scripture does God tell us to make decisions, but He clearly commands us to make disciples. We have missed God's Great Commission if we stop at deciding to trust Christ for salvation. The goal is to move from a decision for Christ to being a disciple of Christ. Baptism is the first step for the believer. Different denominations practice this step in their unique ways, yet God calls us to identify with Him in some form of a public profession of our faith.

As you go and make disciples, I leave you with my personal, biblical definition of discipleship:

> Discipleship is the intentional process whereby forgiven people become faithful followers of Jesus Christ who bear much fruit.[81]

Application:

How do we ensure that we obey the main command of the Great Commission? What are you currently doing to become the disciple that God desires for you to be?

Prayer:

Jesus, I have recently made the decision to repent of my sins and trust You as my Lord and Savior. Thank You for forgiving my sins and saving my soul. Now, I am on a journey to become Your disciple. Train me to learn how to follow You faithfully and consistently...

Day 58

"TEACHING THEM TO OBEY"

Scripture Reading: Matthew 28:20 (NIV)

> *And teaching them to obey everything I have commanded you.*

Explanation:

The fourth verb in the Great Commission is "teaching." The New Testament word means "to cause to learn." When it is found in the Bible, this word almost always refers to the teaching of Scripture. "*Teaching them to obey everything I have commanded you.*" The word "*obey*" in this verse appears seventy-one times in Scripture, and forty-eight of those instances it is translated as "keep." We are to teach people to keep God's commands.

God so desires His followers to make disciples that He doubles the emphasis in His commission. "*Make disciples*" is the primary command of the Great Commission. Then, Jesus commands us to "teach His commands." When you teach His commands, you must teach the main one about making disciples. Since Christ came at it from two directions in His commission, shouldn't we double down on it as His disciples?[82]

Let me illustrate the importance of teaching God's commands. Our military operates on a structure of commands that must be followed to maintain effective order and discipline. Compliance with orders is crucial for achieving success in battle. The safety of every soldier depends on how quickly and thoroughly they follow the commands from their superiors. In military operations, there is no time for explaining why you should carry out instructions. Soldiers know that their life depends on their training and willingness to obey commands.

Paul utilized this soldier analogy in his message to Timothy. Paul wrote: *"No one serving as a soldier gets entangled in civilian affairs but rather tries to please his commanding officer"* (2 Timothy 2:4 NIV). In other words, soldiers don't have time to be worried about what other noncombatants are saying; they simply seek to follow the commands of their superior, who understands the battle.

Likewise, our Lord and Savior suffered a brutal death on the cross. Three days later, He arose from the dead to defeat sin, death, and the grave. Christ understands the battle against our enemy. He fought the devil and won! He is our superior officer. Nobody has more authority than Him. In addition, no one knows the conflict like Christ. That's why He is the One giving the orders. Your success as a believer will be directly connected to how you follow His orders. Rather than asking why, you must simply obey.

You can trust that Jesus will never lead you astray, and He has your best interests at heart. He wants you to experience victory over Satan. The thief comes only to steal, kill, and destroy; Jesus came so that you may have life and have it to the full. (See John 10:10.) Don't miss out on God's best because of disobedience. Double down on becoming His disciple who makes disciples.

Application:

How can you keep God's orders if you don't know what they are? It is essential that we learn His commands so that we can be quick to obey them fully. How important is it to start with the commands found in the Great Commission?

Prayer:

Jesus, thank You for giving me commands in Your Word. It helps me know Your perfect will. As I learn them, help me to obey them. I trust that You know what's best for me…

Day 59

KNOWING HE IS WITH YOU

Scripture Reading: Matthew 28:20 (NIV)

Surely I am with you always, to the very end of the age.

Explanation:

Most people miss the last command of the Great Commission. It is the word *"surely"* in the NIV or *"behold"* in the ESV. In the Greek language, the word is *idou*. It appears 165 times in the New Testament. It means to "look" or "pay careful attention to what follows."[83] Jesus commands us to pay close attention to the fact that He is with us always. The grammatical structure of this phrase double-emphasizes the pronoun "I." Some have translated this to mean "I, even I, will always be with you." God wants you to know that He is present with you. He commands you to see and understand that profound truth.

However, God never said that He would be with you if all you do is live selfishly for yourself. The context of His statement concerning His presence relates to His command to *"make disciples."* "Bless me, Lord, as I ignore Your commands" is not a wise prayer. You can't disobey God and pray that there won't be consequences. Conversely, if you do what God says, He promises never to leave you. You have His word that you will experience His presence when you obey His commands.

Put the truth of God's presence with what you learned from Day 56. Remember Matthew 20:18 NIV: *"All authority in heaven and on earth has been given to me."* We realized that the word "authority" actually means "Out of Who I AM." This is a promise of God's power where Jesus emphasizes the powerful phrase, "*I* AM."

Today, we discovered God's fifth command to behold that He is with us. Again, we see the mighty expression, "*I* AM." Don't you find it extremely interesting that a form of the "*I* AM" statement bookends Jesus's Great Commission? Initially, you are promised His power. In closing, Jesus assures you of His presence.

If that doesn't give you confidence as you live out the Great Commission, I don't know what will! God gives you the command out of all that He is, and Jesus Himself orders you to realize that He will be with you as you carry that command out. If you obey His Great Commission, you cannot fail, because it comes with His power and His presence![84]

As you contemplate Jesus's power and presence, may the following prayer and promise from God's Word give you complete confidence to obey God's command to make disciples.

> *I pray that out of his glorious riches he may strengthen you with power through his Spirit in your inner being, so that Christ may dwell in your hearts through faith. And I pray that you, being rooted and established in love, may have power, together with all the Lord's holy people, to grasp how wide and long and high and deep is the love of Christ, and to know this love that surpasses knowledge—that you may be filled to the measure of all the fullness of God.* (Ephesians 3:16–19 NIV)

> *Be strong and courageous. Do not be afraid or terrified because of them, for the* LORD *your God goes with you; he will never leave you nor forsake you.*
> (Deuteronomy 31:6 NIV)

Application:

How does Jesus's power and presence give you confidence to obey His commands?

Prayer:

Jesus, I know with Your power I can accomplish Your will. And I am sure that since You are with me, I can't lose. Thank You that I never have to walk alone...

Day 60

"YOU WILL BE MY WITNESSES"

Scripture Reading: Acts 1:8 (NIV)

> *But you will receive power when the Holy Spirit comes on you; and you will be my witnesses in Jerusalem, and in all Judea and Samaria, and to the ends of the earth.*

Explanation:

The perfect model for discipleship is Jesus with His first disciples. The next best model of discipleship is the first disciples and the early church. I mean, Jesus is a hard act to follow! He is perfect, and His first followers were blue-collar workers. The real test would be whether the Lord's first disciples could apply the model they learned from Jesus and successfully spread the gospel.

The book of Acts tells us how effectively these first disciples made disciples. It wouldn't be easy. They had obstacles and problems everywhere. Persecution of Christians was rampant. Jesus had been crucified, which put fear into all who associated with His name! Then there was the sheer magnitude of the task at hand. Have you ever heard someone in church leadership say, "We just grew too fast to have time to make disciples"? Look at all the challenges the early church overcame to make disciples.

In Acts 1, Jesus instructed His disciples to remain in Jerusalem and promised them that the Holy Spirit would come. Waiting was their first test. Do you know anyone who likes to wait? I mean, just a few verses later, they ask Him about the timing of everything! Jesus's response in Acts 1:7 was short and to the point, *"It is not for you to know the times or dates the Father has set by his own authority"* (NIV). These first disciples had to trust that if God said it, that settles it! His Word was all that they needed as instructions.

Then Jesus gave His disciples one final marching order: *"But you will receive power when the Holy Spirit comes on you; and you will be my witnesses in Jerusalem, and in all Judea and Samaria, and to the ends of the earth"* (Acts 1:8 NIV).

Jesus basically moved them in their thinking from worrying about *when,* to focusing on *Who* will be with them each step of the journey. We get so caught up in times and places that we miss His truth and the power of the Holy Spirit that indwells us and surrounds us.

Then, Jesus ascended into heaven before their very eyes. God sent two angels to challenge them for standing there, looking up into the sky. The angels told the disciples that Jesus would return in the same way He had ascended. Translation: "Get to work. Quit standing around. He's coming back one day!"

So, the disciples obeyed the word of the Lord and go back to Jerusalem. They went to the Upper Room and joined together constantly in prayer. Then, Peter stood before the group that had gathered and quoted Scripture from Psalm 69:25 and Psalm 109:8. Approximately 120 people were present. Then, in Acts 2, the Holy Spirit that Jesus had promised in Acts 1 fell on the people. Peter got up and preached the death, burial, and resurrection of Jesus. He called for people to repent and be baptized, and 3,000 people were saved and added to the church that day! I would love to have been in that worship service! Talk about fast church growth. How do you handle 3,000 additions in one day?

Yet, Acts 2 ends with a description of how the church lived out its faith! They made disciples who made disciples.[85] It is God's plan to grow His church. Salvation leads to discipleship. So, go and be His witnesses and tell others what God has done!

Application:

In what ways can you apply what you have learned to your daily walk with the Lord? How will you live out God's will for your life?

Prayer:

Jesus, thank You for this walk of faith. It is only the beginning of my journey with You, but I am excited for what's next....

CONCLUSION

Congratulations! You are on the right path to becoming a disciple of Jesus Christ. Never forget that being a disciple means you are a continual learner. Jesus is the Master Teacher, and there is always something new to learn about Him and your Christian journey. The longer you walk with Christ, the more you should know Him. The more you know Him, the greater your love will be for your Lord, Savior, and Friend. A relationship with Jesus is an ever-progressing journey that is thrilling, transforming, and fulfilling.

The goal of *Seven Minutes with Jesus for New Believers* was to start your day thinking about Jesus Christ by reading just a small portion of His Word and seeking to apply one additional truth from Scripture to your life. Hopefully, these seven minutes in God's Word have caused a chain reaction of godly thoughts that helped you focus on God's will throughout your day. May these last sixty days lead to a daily focus on Jesus that directs you to God's best for your life.

Don't ever settle for less than God's best for you. You will always have as much of Jesus as you want. Keep your desire strong for Jesus and stay passionately in love with Him. Remember, He has greater plans for your life than you have for your own.

Prayer:

Jesus, I worship You for being a personal God who allows me to know You and be known by You. Thank You for these last sixty days, and I praise You in advance for what lies ahead...

ABOUT THE AUTHOR

Dr. Ray Cummings has pastored churches in Mississippi and Alabama for over eighteen years and has been in ministry for over thirty years. He resides in Purvis, Mississippi, and serves as senior pastor at Hattiesburg Community Church. He graduated from William Carey College in 1992 with a bachelor's degree in pre-med. He attended New Orleans Baptist Theological Seminary, where he received a master of divinity with languages degree in 1996 and a doctor of ministry specializing in church growth and evangelism in 2001.

He has been married to his partner in ministry, Amanda Burge Cummings, since December 6, 1997. They have three sons: Carter, who is married to Hope; Camron; and Moses, along with one daughter named Mercy. Ray loves preaching, writing, hunting, and anything sports-related.

ENDNOTES

1. Martin B. Copenhaver, *Jesus Is the Question: The 307 Questions Jesus Asked and the 3 He Answered* (Nashville: Abingdon Press, 2014).

2. Ray Cummings, *Seven Minutes with Jesus for Men: Applying the Gospel of John to Everyday Life* (New Kensington, PA: Whitaker House, 2025), 5–6.

3. Jocelyn Solis-Moreira, "How Long Does It Really Take to Form a Habit?" *Scientific American*, February 20, 2024, https://www.scientificamerican.com/article/how-long-does-it-really-take-to-form-a-habit/.

4. "Strong's Greek: 4161. ποίημα (*poiēma*)—Workmanship, Creation, Work," *Bible Hub*, accessed October 9, 2025, https://biblehub.com/greek/4161.htm.

5. "Strong's Greek: 26. ἀγάπη (*agapē*)—Love," *Bible Hub*, accessed October 9, 2025, https://biblehub.com/greek/26.htm.

6. "Strong's Greek: 1097. γινώσκω (*ginōskō*)—To Know, To Come to Know, To Recognize, To Perceive," *Bible Hub*, accessed October 9, 2025, https://biblehub.com/greek/1097.htm.

7. Charles R. Swindoll, *Insights on 1, 2 & 3 John, Jude*, vol. 14 of *Swindoll's Living Insights New Testament Commentary* (Carol Stream, IL: Tyndale House Publishers, 2018).

8. "Strong's Greek: 5048. τελειόω (*teleioō*)—To Complete, To Perfect, To Accomplish, To Bring to an End," *Bible Hub*, accessed October 9, 2025, https://biblehub.com/greek/5048.htm.

9. "Strong's Greek: 3954. παρρησία (*parrēsia*)—Boldness, Confidence, Openness, Plainness," *Bible Hub*, accessed October 9, 2025, https://biblehub.com/greek/3954.htm.

10. Corrie Ten Boom, "Corrie Ten Boom Quote," *QuoteFancy*, accessed October 9, 2025, https://quotefancy.com/quote/789887.

11. "Strong's Greek: 8475 Self-Denial—Dictionary of Bible Themes," *Bible Gateway*, accessed October 9, 2025, https://www.biblegateway.com/resources/dictionary-of-bible-themes/8475-self-denial.

12. R. C. Sproul, *A Walk with God: An Exposition of Luke* (Great Britain: Christian Focus Publications, 1999).

13. Bruce B. Barton, David Veerman, Linda Chaffee Taylor, and Grant R. Osborne, *Luke, Life Application Bible Commentary* (Wheaton, IL: Tyndale House Publishers, 1997).

14. Ron Edmondson, "7 Excuses for Not Doing What God Has Called Us to Do," *RonEdmondson.com*, December 12, 2018, https://ronedmondson.com/2018/12/7-best-excuses-we-make.html.

15. Greg Stier, "Top 10 Biggest Excuses for Not Sharing the Gospel," *GregStier.org*, March 22, 2023, https://gregstier.org/top-10-biggest-excuses-for-not-sharing-the-gospel/.

16. Charles M. Sheldon, *In His Steps* (Uhrichsville, OH: Barbour Books, 2020).

17. "Strong's Greek: 5261. ὑπογραμμός (*hupogrammos*)—Example, Pattern," *Bible Hub*, accessed October 9, 2025, https://biblehub.com/greek/5261.htm.

18. Frazer Church, *In His Steps* (Montgomery, AL: Frazer Discipleship, 2024), 1–2.

19. R. C. Sproul, *Can I Know God's Will?*, vol. 4 of *The Crucial Questions Series* (Lake Mary, FL: Reformation Trust Publishing, 2009).

20. Raymond C. Ortlund Jr., *Proverbs—Wisdom That Works, Preaching the Word* series, ed. R. Kent Hughes (Wheaton, IL: Crossway, 2012).

21. Ibid.

22. "Strong's Greek: 2307. θέλημα (*thelēma*)—Will, Desire, Purpose," *Bible Hub*, accessed October 9, 2025, https://biblehub.com/greek/2307.htm.

23. "Strong's Greek: 38. ἁγιασμός (*hagiasmos*)—Sanctification, Holiness, Consecration," *Bible Hub*, accessed October 9, 2025, https://biblehub.com/greek/38.htm.

24. Tom Wright, *Paul for Everyone: Galatians and Thessalonians* (London: Society for Promoting Christian Knowledge, 2004).

25. Ben Witherington III, *1 and 2 Thessalonians: A Socio-Rhetorical Commentary* (Grand Rapids, MI: Wm. B. Eerdmans Publishing Co., 2006).

26. "1 Thessalonians 5:16," *Bible Hub Interlinear*, accessed October 9, 2025, https://biblehub.com/interlinear/1_thessalonians/5-16.htm.

27. "1 Thessalonians 5," *Bible Hub Interlinear*, accessed October 9, 2025, https://biblehub.com/interlinear/1_thessalonians/5.htm.

28. "Strong's Greek: 4336. προσεύχομαι (*proseuchomai*)—To Pray," *Bible Hub*, accessed October 9, 2025, https://biblehub.com/greek/4336.htm.

29. "Pray Without Ceasing," *City Harvest AG Church Bangalore*, November 14, 2023, https://cityharvestag.com/sermons/pray-without-ceasing.

30. "John Wesley on 'Pray Without Ceasing,'" *Wesleyan Life*, accessed October 9, 2025, https://wesleyan.life/john-wesley-on-pray-without-ceasing.

31. D. Britton, "Let's Pray Real Quick," *Fellowship of Christian Athletes Blog*, September 28, 2023, https://www.fca.org/fca-in-action/blog-detail/2023/09/28/let's-pray-real-quick.

32. Chris Hodges, *Pray First: The Transformative Power of a Life Built on Prayer* (Nashville: Thomas Nelson, 2022).

33. Billy Graham, "Prayer Is Simply...," *BrainyQuote*, accessed October 9, 2025, https://www.brainyquote.com/quotes/billy_graham_382920.

34. Charles Stanley, *Prayer: The Ultimate Conversation*, accessed October 9, 2025, https://www.goodreads.com/book/show/18942920-prayer.

35. Bruce B. Barton, *Matthew, Life Application Bible Commentary* (Wheaton, IL: Tyndale House Publishers, 1996).

36. Charles R. Swindoll, *Luke*, vol. 3 of *Swindoll's Living Insights New Testament Commentary* (Carol Stream, IL: Tyndale House Publishers, 2017).

37. R. C. Sproul, *A Walk with God: An Exposition of Luke* (Great Britain: Christian Focus Publications, 1999).

38. "Strong's Greek: 37. ἁγιάζω (*hagiazō*)—To Sanctify, To Make Holy, To Consecrate, To Set Apart," *Bible Hub*, accessed October 9, 2025, https://biblehub.com/greek/37.htm.

39. Lewis B. Smedes, "Lewis B. Smedes — To Forgive Is to Set a Prisoner Free and Discover That the Prisoner Was You," *BrainyQuote*, accessed October 9, 2025, https://www.brainyquote.com/quotes/lewis_b_smedes_135524.

40. Douglas Sean O'Donnell, *Matthew: All Authority in Heaven and on Earth, Preaching the Word* series, ed. R. Kent Hughes (Wheaton, IL: Crossway, 2013).

41. Martin Luther, "To Be a Christian...," *BrainyQuote*, accessed October 9, 2025, https://www.brainyquote.com/quotes/martin_luther_385793.

42.Billy Graham, "True Prayer Is a Way of Life...," *Goodreads*, accessed October 9, 2025, https://www.goodreads.com/quotes/7485758-true-prayer-is-a-way-of-life-not-just-for.

43. "Strong's Greek: 2315. θεόπνευστος (*theopneustos*)—God-Breathed, Inspired by God," *Bible Hub*, accessed October 9, 2025, https://biblehub.com/greek/2315.htm.

44. Warren W. Wiersbe, *Be Exultant*, 1st ed., "Be" Commentary Series (Colorado Springs, CO: Cook Communications Ministries, 2004).

45. "Strong's Greek: 5624. ὠφέλιμος (*ōphelimos*)—Profitable, Beneficial, Useful," *Bible Hub*, accessed October 9, 2025, https://biblehub.com/greek/5624.htm.

46. "Strong's Hebrew: 2656. חֵפֶץ (*chephets*)—Delight, Pleasure, Desire, Purpose, Matter," *Bible Hub*, accessed October 9, 2025, https://biblehub.com/hebrew/2656.htm.

47. "Strong's Hebrew: 1697. דָּבָר (*dābār*)—Word, Matter, Thing, Speech, Command, Promise," *Bible Hub*, accessed October 9, 2025, https://biblehub.com/hebrew/1697.htm.

48. "Strong's Hebrew: 3176. יָחַל (*yāchal*)—To Wait, Hope, Expect," *Bible Hub*, accessed October 9, 2025, https://biblehub.com/hebrew/3176.htm.

49. Ron Rhodes, *1001 Unforgettable Quotes about God, Faith, & the Bible* (Eugene, OR: Harvest House Publishers, 2011).

50. "Strong's Greek: 1247. διακονέω (*diakoneō*)—To Serve, To Minister, To Attend To," *Bible Hub*, accessed October 9, 2025, https://biblehub.com/greek/1247.htm.

51. "Strong's Greek: 1398. δουλεύω (*douleuō*)—To Serve, To Be a Slave To, To Be in Bondage," *Bible Hub*, accessed October 9, 2025, https://biblehub.com/greek/1398.htm.

52. "Strong's Greek: 5257. ὑπηρέτης (*hypēretēs*)—Servant, Attendant, Minister, Officer," *Bible Hub*, accessed October 9, 2025, https://biblehub.com/greek/5257.htm.

53. Ray Cummings, *From Decisions to Disciples: Obeying the Divine Command* (Published by the Author, 2023), 83–84.

54. "Strong's Greek: 5426. φρονέω (*phroneō*)—To Think, To Set One's Mind On, To Have a Mindset," *Bible Hub*, accessed October 9, 2025, https://biblehub.com/greek/5426.htm.

55. "Strong's Greek: 1401. δοῦλος (*doulos*)—Servant, Slave, Bondservant," *Bible Hub*, accessed October 9, 2025, https://biblehub.com/greek/1401.htm.

56. "Strong's Greek: 3083. λύτρον (*lytron*)—Ransom, Redemption Price," *Bible Hub*, accessed October 9, 2025, https://biblehub.com/greek/3083.htm.

57. "Strong's Greek: 3107. μακάριος (*makarios*)—Blessed, Happy, Fortunate," *Bible Hub*, accessed October 9, 2025, https://biblehub.com/greek/3107.htm.

58. Bruce B. Barton, *Matthew, Life Application Bible Commentary* (Wheaton, IL: Tyndale House Publishers, 1996).

59. A. W. Tozer, "Top 25 Servant of God Quotes," *AZ Quotes*, accessed October 9, 2025, https://www.azquotes.com/quotes/topics/servant-of-god.html.

60. Warren W. Wiersbe, *The Bible Exposition Commentary*, vol. 1 (Wheaton, IL: Victor Books, 1996).

61. Rick Warren, "Top 25 Servant of God Quotes," *AZ Quotes*, accessed October 9, 2025, https://www.azquotes.com/quotes/topics/servant-of-god.html.

62. J. I. Packer, "J. I. Packer Quote," *AZ Quotes*, accessed October 9, 2025, https://www.azquotes.com/quote/532815.

63. Ray Cummings, *From Decisions to Disciples: Obeying the Divine Command* (Published by the Author, 2023), 53–56.

64. Warren W. Wiersbe, *Real Worship: Playground, Battleground, or Holy Ground?* (Grand Rapids, MI: Baker Books, n.d.), 20, 183, 216.

65. Ibid.

66. A. W. Tozer, "30 Great Quotes on Worship," *Experiencing Worship*, February 25, 2024, https://www.experiencingworship.com/articles/general/2001-7-great-quotes-on-worship.html.

67. Leon Morris, *The Epistle to the Romans, The Pillar New Testament Commentary* (Grand Rapids, MI; Leicester, England: W. B. Eerdmans; Inter-Varsity Press, 1988).

68. Edward Rowell, ed., *1001 Quotes, Illustrations, and Humorous Stories: For Preachers, Teachers and Writers* (Grand Rapids, MI: Baker Publishing Group, 2008).

69. Ray Cummings, *From Decisions to Disciples: Obeying the Divine Command* (Published by the Author, 2023), 35–37.

70. "Strong's Greek: 2842. κοινωνία (koinōnia)—Fellowship, Communion, Participation, Sharing," Bible Hub, accessed October 9, 2025, https://biblehub.com/greek/2842.htm.

71. "Strong's Greek: 2657. κατανοέω (*katanoeō*)—To Observe, Consider, Perceive, Understand," *Bible Hub*, accessed October 9, 2025, https://biblehub.com/greek/2657.htm.

72. "Strong's Greek: 3948. παροξυσμός (*paroxysmos*)—Provocation, Stirring Up, Sharp Disagreement," *Bible Hub*, accessed October 9, 2025, https://biblehub.com/greek/3948.htm.

73. George Sweeting, *Who Said That? More than 2,500 Usable Quotes and Illustrations* (Chicago, IL: Moody Publishers, 1995).

74. Ibid.

75. Cummings, *From Decisions to Disciples*, 16.

76. Strong's Greek: 1411. δύναμις (*dunamis*)—Power, Strength, Ability, Might, Miracle," *Bible Hub*, accessed October 9, 2025, https://biblehub.com/greek/1411.htm.

77. Strong's Greek: 1849. ἐξουσία (*exousia*)—Authority, power, right, jurisdiction," *Bible Hub*, accessed October 9, 2025, https://biblehub.com/greek/1849.htm.

78. Cummings, *From Decisions to Disciples*, 16–17.

79. Strong's Greek: 3100. μαθητεύω (*mathéteuó*)—To make a disciple, to teach, to instruct," *Bible Hub*, accessed October 9, 2025, https://biblehub.com/greek/3100.htm.

80. Cummings, *From Decisions to Disciples*, 18–19.

81. Cummings, *From Decisions to Disciples*, 22.

82. Cummings, *From Decisions to Disciples*, 19–20.

83. "Strong's Greek: 2400. ἰδού (*idou*)—Behold, Look, See," *Bible Hub*, accessed October 9, 2025, https://biblehub.com/greek/2400.htm.

84. Cummings, *From Decisions to Disciples*, 17.

85. Cummings, *From Decisions to Disciples*, 32–35.